The Blood of JESUS
As Our Healer

A thesis paper submitted in partial fulfillment
of the requirement for the Degree of
Master of Biblical Studies and Theology
Minnesota Graduate School of Theology
April 17, 2007
Approved by Sam B. Gutierrez, ThD
Director of Education, South Texas Bible Institute

DELRAY SHUDARK, M.A.

ISBN 978-1-0980-7343-5 (paperback)
ISBN 978-1-0980-7344-2 (digital)

Christian Faith Publishing, Inc.
832 Park Avenue
Meadville, PA 16335
www.christianfaithpublishing.com

Printed in the United States of America

Introduction

As humans, we are often concerned about our health, and as Christians, we often think about whether or not we are living a good life. We also wonder if what we are doing is what God desires for us. As we take a look at the blood of Jesus as our healer, we must start with the beginning of creation when God spoke His words, the very words that activated life. God needed a companion to fellowship with, so He created man. How God gets feedback is from the members of His body. What Spiritual substance, as well as fleshly substance, makes up Jesus's body? The answer is the same image that man was made. What is the source of blood flow, which was poured out for us? Also knowing what and where we are looking for our healing and what the sure source of healing is. When we know the source, then we can draw from that living spirit provided by Jesus with truth. In our lifetime, one has had many false healers that say this is what you need to do. We are to remember He came to the earth as the Son of man. Jesus had to have a body for the substance of the Holy Spirit to walk on earth, and at the same time, it was the Holy Spirit implanted within Mary that caused her to conceive. The body used to conceive the Spirit had to be pure; we are also to keep our bodies pure and healthy so the Holy Spirit will be able to do what is needed in our life. Our blood is from Adam and sin was upon Him. One would do good to ask, what other traits did we inherit from Adam? He was made in the image of the Father, Son, and Holy Spirit. There is fleshly body blood and there is the pure blood (purified by the Holy Spirit). All throughout this writing, we will make reference to blood and understand which blood it is, pure blood of Jesus or the fleshly sinful blood of Adam. Salvation through pure blood has to takes place; this is the blood transfusion we receive when we proclaim Jesus as our Lord. Proclaiming Jesus as Lord washes us in the blood of Jesus for total healing unto salvation. Throughout this paper, we will see why the blood that heals us leads us to salvation and is good for us right now in this day and hour. We will see why the elements of creation of the body and the blood are related to the elements of creation that are found in the dirt. We will understand that God planted a harvest and be able to understand why He planted it. We will be able to understand the beginning of blood formation from our fleshly body and understand all that the blood does for us right now. We will look at our blood in our bodies before salvation, and then compare it to the exception of the blood by confession of Him as our Lord, and by accepting Him into all areas of our life for healing. This will lead us into oneness with our Creator, predestined from the beginning of creation waiting for His children to partake in all of His grace and mercy. God wants us home with Him. This will lead us to a deep understanding of why we are not to leave out the blood in any area of our worship of God. Without blood that is moving and flowing from part to part of the Lord's body, there will not be a healthy body of Christ (the church). We believers are all going to assemble our part with the other parts to make up the one body of Christ. The Lord's will is to rise up and see to it that His children are on the right path with Him into the new heaven and new earth. The Lord will always be there to help us when we call out to Him and give Him honor that is due His name. Our bodies were intimately made and every thought went into creation of it even down to the very breath that God was breathing.

Acknowledgments

I have known Delray for some twenty-plus years. We met at a Promise Keepers event in Dallas, Texas, I know Delray has a heart for God. Looking to serve the Kingdom and help individuals to see the path that God has for each of us. His character has never wavered. He is a man of integrity. It makes my heart jump for joy in that he will share an honest perspective of the Blood and how it will transform you.

Sincerely,
Your Brother in Christ
DJ Jantz

I have had the privilege of knowing Delray Shudark for over twenty-five years. As one of his pastors, I have watched him grow in Christ and his love for the word of God.

Delray is married to his beautiful wife, Sharon, for thirty-five years, and they have four children. He was born again and surrendered his life to Christ in 1995. He immediately jumped in and has served in many outreaches and ministry of help departments her at Cornerstone Church. From Walk to Emmaus, Promise Keepers, Standing in the Gap at Washington, DC, Ushering, Children's Ministry Master Teacher, and Prison Ministry, he excels in all!

Delray graduated with his master's degree from South Texas Bible Institute, and his thesis was the introduction for the writing of this book. He has a heart to see people come to know Jesus Christ as their personal savior and to continually grow in their relationship with the Lord.

His sense of humor and unique was of seeing and relating things are two traits we have grown to love about Delray. I think you will too as you start your journey with this book.

Enjoy and grow in Him,
Rev. Catherine I. Smith, MA
Cornerstone Church
PO Box 18683
Corpus Christi, TX 78480-8683

Thesis Statement

At the creation of man, there was a Spirit formed first in the image of God. That Spirit was with God and in His likeness. Later, a body with blood and all other elements was formed for man from the dirt of the earth. Then there was a combination of both the body and spirit by adding of the breath of life from God. This writing will address the form of the earthly body we have and the preparation of the heavenly body that we as children of God inherit. It will address the changes that the body is faced with while on earth. When Adam sinned, this removed the covering of the spirit and changed the environment around his body. The sin around him changed the protection of the body's elements against the sinful nature he lives in apart from the Garden of Eden. God sent His Son Jesus to restore our body's environment from sin and add the protection back that it once had. This is done by the shedding of Jesus's purified blood on the cross. If we believe that Jesus died and rose again and take Him into our heart, then we will activate the love of restoration for our body into the state that it was meant to live. The conditioning of the body on earth will prepare us to live in the heavenly realm with the Father. Becoming a believer will guarantee that we live out our life in eternity with God. This writing will point out some inherited Blood elements that were inherited from Adam and how they are interwoven with the Blood elements that will take us to the throne room of the Father and the place of the final offering set before Him. This writing will also point out that all living things have life, but it is life with the Spirit included that we get our salvation and are saved. We will see that being in right standing with God will guarantee our oneness and put the heavenly body of Christ into the fullness of His glory.

The Blood Elements
of Created Life

What does Jesus's blood heal us from? Why did He shed all that blood for us? Why did God create our bodies? We need to understand what we are made up from and the whole starting of the life process. Why is there so much misunderstanding about what blood does: what it did then and what it is doing for our lives now? What is it that we need to feed on that will lead us to understanding our healer and His healing process for our life? When we know in whom we are made and the reason we were made, then we will be able to figure out that we were made with a special flow of blood elements. The life-giving blood elements react with the breath of life which was blown into the first created human body and what Adam's descendents inherited generations later. Often one tries to figure out what all took place, but only God knew. Every breath we take is a renewing of life, as new oxygen removes old used oxygen from our blood in the form of carbon dioxide. Keeping our bodies healthy is one thing, but what about the Spirit in the inner being of man? The Spiritual container (our body) must be healthy to be able to house the power of the Holy Spirit. In the Garden of Eden, the body and Spirit was all together as one contained within Adam. Just like our heart is connected to our bodies, so was the fruit connected to the vine. After Eve offered Adam a bad offering, there was a body and Spiritual change. There was now a distances between God because of the choice of fruit that was picked. This distance was because Eve picked the tree of the knowledge of good and evil. The true way the body should operate is to operate under the covering of the tree of life. When the body is affected, then the blood is affected also. Now Adam is in need of renewing with the Holy Spirit and power because sin has changed his environment. Satan deceived Eve to get to Adam; Adam allowed the bad spirit of Satan to control his thoughts. Satan looked for a weak area for temptations in the flesh. But there was a plan in place by God to return the environment to its original state by sending Jesus. Just the thought of our Father God sending His Son for us to be healed is amazing. He sent His Son because His Son's blood was the same blood as His image. God knew that His Son would be exposed to many different diseases and to the sins that had a hold on the earth. All the sin went against what God originally planned for man; this in turn infected the bodies and hearts of the people and paradise seem lost. There was no one who could restore the paradise on earth as well as the one in heaven, but Jesus. God prepared a mansion with many rooms just for us, he made our room especially for us, and we need to make room for Him in our house. I have three sons, and it would be very hard for me to say that. I'm going to send one of them into an area that is in a condition such as earth. Our Father God knew the power of the blood because it is incorruptible. To understand our healer, we must become intimate with Jesus. How do we get this intimate relationship? It's a free gift, if one only believes in Him. Being intimate will also make sure we are healed in all areas of your life. Often, one believes that they are in rightful standing already, when really they are far from the mark. We must ask: what does Jesus feed on to keep Himself healthy? What elements are in the food Jesus is filled with? Can we as children bless and feed the Lord back? Yes. We are a product of the Spiritual elements and earthly elements. Where do the elements that Jesus has come from? From Jesus's Father who is in heaven and on earth. Have you heard that saying "You are what you eat?" It would be fair to say that if the Lord plants a harvest, it is for Him to feed on. This is the principle of seed time and harvest. Did you ever know of a farmer that plants a harvest and didn't partake of the increase come harvest time? A good chef will taste his own recipe to make sure it is good enough to be served. There is also the baker's dozen which is thirteen, one extra to sample that which was prepared. Understanding our recipe of elements in the blood will also help us understand the Lord's will for us to be healed. Our blood is made up from the different vitamins and elements that are in the food we put into our bodies. I choose to feed on the Lord's recipe for food so I will not get spiritual hungry again. If we never hunger, then we should not be hungry and will not eat the foods that make us sick. I chose to receive all of the Father's blessings that are available when I partake in the blood and body of Jesus. There is a grand recipe meal that is sitting at the Father's table if we choose to dine with Him. It says that the Lord will send forth laborers into His harvest. Who is it that's sending forth laborers into the harvest? The answer is the Lord is sending them. Our meals are to be made up of what His harvest provides.

> "Then saith he unto his disciples, the harvest truly is plenteous, but the laborers, are few; Pray ye therefore the Lord of the harvest, that he will send forth laborers into his harvest" (Matthew 9:37–38 KJV).

Along with the meal He gives us, His living water to drink. First the blood poured out of Jesus, then the water poured out while on the cross, it was His all poured out for us.

> "As Jesus made his way toward Galilee he came to Jacob's Well in Samaria. Weary from the journey, he stopped to rest there while his disciples went to buy food; In the meantime, a Samaritan woman came to the well to draw water. Jesus made a simple request of her, 'Give me to drink'" (John 4:7 KJV).

> "Christ's words to the woman began a long conversation. She ended up talking at length, and so did Jesus. During their talk she was amazed at

the things he told her, Finally she said, 'I know that the Messiah cometh, which is called Christ; when he is come, he will tell us all things, Jesus saith unto her, I that speak unto thee am he'" (John 4:25–26 KJV).

"Just as Christ revealed his identity to her, the disciples returned. They were amazed to find their master so deeply engaged in conversation with this Samaritan woman. As they sat to prepare a meal, the wide-eyes woman hurried back to town. Finally; when the food was ready, they said, 'Master, eat'" (John 4:31 KJV).

"Jesus responded with this puzzling statement: 'I have meat to eat that ye know not of'" (John 4:32 KJV).

He was telling them in essence, "I've already been fed, and my food is not of this world." Here we are learning what Jesus feeds on. If the food that feeds Him is not of this world, why are we feeding only on what this world has to offer? Satan is trying to get us to feed on what he has to offer. Jesus cares for our bodies and wants us to only receive His goodness; God made Adam's body, Soul, and Spirit in His image. What was God's image at that point? He was Spirit. Jesus told his disciples, in essence, "My hunger has been met by this Samaritan woman." She brought me an honest seeking heart Jesus was fed by an honest seeking heart, so we see how important the elements of our heart activity are. From the very beginning, we see the Lord seeking communion with man.

His Spirit walked with Adam in the Garden of Eden, conversing in the cool of the day. These intimate times were food to the Lord, delighting and pleasing to Him because He said, "His hunger has been met." Such fellowship was His plan from the beginning. Now we see that fellowship feeds Him also and He walks with us is

His delight. The book of Genesis talks about a man named Enoch being taken to heaven:

"Enoch walked with God and he was not; for God took him" (Genesis 5:24). Enoch had communed with the Lord for 365 years. Yet he lived only half the normal life-span at that time. Why do you think God brought Enoch to glory so soon? His peers lived to be seven- and eight-hundred years old. Why would God take him during midlife? I have no answer. The Spirit whispered fellowship is my food; Enoch communed with me, waiting on me, getting to know my voice. He listened as I opened my heart to him. Our fellowship became so intimate; I wanted him with me in eternity. What about Moses? He communed with me as no other man did. Why do you think he came back from the mount with a supernatural glow on his face? It was the effect of being in my presence, for forty days and nights. When we met face to face, he fed me."[1] In the World Challenge Publication, we see how Jesus is fed. For in Him we live, and move, and have our being: as certain also of your own poets have said, for we are also his offspring. God will always make sure that we are being fed with His never ending yield of blessings.

> "I will send you such a blessing in the sixth year that the land will yield enough for three years, while you plant during the eighth year, you will eat from the old crop and will continue to eat from it until the harvest of the ninth year come in" (Lev 25:21–22 NIV Thompson chain reference Bible).

God sends a harvest that is essential for health and nourishment that will build up our blood and keep our fleshly immune system healthy, as well as our Spiritual immune system strong. God wants us to be immune to the sinfulness of Satan, which is why He is providing a three-year harvest return before the rest period. This is saying

---

[1] World Challenge, Inc. Feeding Christ, Feb 13, 2002.

the field is to rest in the seventh year. During the seventh year, it is then time to reseed the land or to place seed everywhere you plan on getting a return. God planted a harvest of seed for His return, which was us, His seed. The Lord is giving us time to plant His spiritual seed in the right soil of our heart. We need to know what elements are keeping us healthy. We are to be in the state of mind to return blessing and keep the Lord's body healthy. But God said in Lev 21–22, there is a never-ending crop, because in the sixth year, the yield last three more years. Even when the field was at rest the seventh year, there was return from the seeds planted in the sixth year. There are times when we just may not feel healthy, so we are to remember the seed of God's love that was planted long ago. There is an overlapping harvest so the Lord is making sure His elements of food and healing is never ending. Often we feel as though we are feeding on the same old harvest, but wait, there is a fresh harvest yield coming. Are you storing up an offering back to the Lord for His complete harvest return, when all the right elements are in proper order, then He will say you fed me? The circle of love and healing will be complete when we return our harvest back to Him. We have all come from the Lord's image which explains where the healing is. He gave so much; we are to give some back through our tithe, fellowship, prayer, and having an intimate relationship with Him in return. He is our only true God that has our freedom at heart, given to us to worship Him back with. Praise God for my life-giving elements that bring good health and family health to keep the Lord's body healthy in return.

> "All things were made by him, and without him was not anything made that was made" (John 1:3 KJV, AMP).

It is very important that our bodies feed on the right nutrients. Let us look at some of those nutrients. He made our bodies from the elements found in the dirt of the earth, which he spoke and His words formed. We were not created by anyone else because He was the only one who knew all the elements that were needed to create our soul. He has the whole world in His hands (I created). His words were spoken, so therefore it was.

God always has a purpose for doing something. I truly believe that there was a reason for dirt to be the choice of the creation of man. The dirt of creation was from within the Garden of Eden, God's pure and holy creation. When we look at the breakdown of elements in the blood and not just the blood as a whole, then we can come to more of an understanding of what the blood does for us. Being outside the garden, one is exposed to the polluted elements of sin. God said, "If you turn from sin I'll heal your land." We were created outside of the Garden. What are our body and spirit elements?[2] Tissue nutrient minerals such as calcium, magnesium, sodium, potassium, iron, copper, manganese, zinc, chromium, selenium, and phosphorus, and there are additional minerals (nickel, cobalt, molybdenium, lithium, boron). Let's look at the elements of the blood and the dirt of creation and how they are related. Oxygen and hydrogen combined make up 46 percent of the earth's surface, which is water. Our bodies contain more than 90 percent water.

Calcium is the fifth most abundant element, an important nutrient of bones. In your lifetime, you'll lose about 600 bones! Before you were born, your skeleton contained over 800 separate bones, many of which grew or fused together so that you had about 450 at birth. By age 20, when your bones have finished growing and the separate parts have fused together, they'll number only about 206.[3] The milk we drink has calcium that enters the blood stream for our bones to grow. We become stronger fleshly as we start to eat more solid earthly food. Our spiritual strength must come from spiritual food from the Word of God. Jesus's blood helps us fuse together with the Father's through the restoring of our human reaction to pain. Father God wants us to grow up spiritually, strengthen ourselves and grow together in one body (the church) of God. We are to treat our bodies with goodness and not evil desires that stops the healing process.

---

[2]   Analytical Research Labs Inc, Tissue Mineral Analysis.
[3]   Stephen Cubaa, The Bones and Skeletdn Book.

"Anyone who lives on milk, being still an infant is not acquainted with the teaching about righteousness, but solid food is for the mature, who by constant use have trained themselves to distinguish good from evil" (Heb 5:13 KJV).

When we all grow up and feed on the Spiritual food, it renews the blood counts that result in healing. One can say we can count on God for renewing. Let us look at the container of an infant's body compared to an adult's container. Normal red blood cell counts vary, depending on the type of sample and on the person's age and sex. Full-term infants have 4.4 to 5.8 million red blood cells per micro liter of blood at birth, decreasing to 3 to 3.8 million at age 2 months and decreasing slowly thereafter. A newborn's red blood count is more than that of an adult man. Let our bodily container remain full of the Salvation blood of Jesus that leads to eternity with Him.

"Like newborn born babies, crave pure spiritual milk, so that by it you may grow up in your salvation, now that you have tasted that the Lord is good" (1 Peter 2:2 KJV).

A newborn's blood mass per size of its body is 55 percent to 68 percent, and it has more bones; this means more bone marrow. The adult male has 42 percent to 54 percent, and an adult female 38 percent to 46 percent.[4] The woman is known as the weaker vessel. A rib bone was removed from Adam to make the first woman Eve, and the rib bone contains marrow that produced the body's blood cells. This also took place while in the Garden. Just before a person's birth, all the woman's marrow-producing bones produce more red blood cells. This super abundant of red cells produced before birth activates protection. The marrow of the sternum, ribs, the vertebrae (back bone), and pelvis (hips) produce the most red cells. The entire bone structure put together make up the support system that supports our soul,

---

4   Springhouse, Everything You Need To Know About Medical Test.

spirit, and mind. Where do we get our power to stand up to the devil and his schemes? We get it from the support of God through His son Jesus for us. We are all children of God. The devil doesn't have any bone or blood marrow-producing bones that produce healing power for us, for he is a fallen angel. Let us look at the elements of dirt and the elements of blood. The devil can't produce anything with life that is why he is trying to steal, kill, and destroy our life. Satan doesn't want us to have power. Satan can only use words against us in our brain thoughts. Yet a lot of people don't believe in God for their healing and look somewhere else; there is nowhere else to look. Often, people on their own will end up not finding truth for their life. Here are some of the elements that found in dirt and blood that are related to creation and healing of our life.

Magnesium is the seventh most abundant element. It is found in seawater. (Plasma is a salty watery substance.) Plasma activates several substances called enzymes.

Sodium is reactive, producing heat when mixed with water (Refiner's fire).

Potassium is a major electrolyte that helps regulates acid-base balance and neuromuscular function. A potassium imbalance may cause a person to have muscle weakness, nausea, diarrhea, confusion, low blood pressure, and electrocardiogram changes.

Iron is an element that absorbs more energy than it releases. Jesus will never run out of energy for healing. He wants us to always be absorbing more of him daily.

Copper is an element that transmits electrical energy and is used to kill various forms of fungi and bacteria. We need to keep plugged into the power source of Jesus's blood for our brain activity to transmit correctly. Plead the blood of Jesus over your home, land, and the environment you live and work in, so that you are not polluted with the bacteria and fungi of the world.

Manganese has magnetic properties and makes steel harder (iron sharpens iron). We can keep the sword of the word sharp by accepting the blood. Manganese is also a battery compound. We are to keep charged up with the Word of God and know who the true power source is.

Zinc protects from corrosion (Jesus poured out his blood to stop us from eternal and internal corrosion). Zinc plays a critical role in maintaining good health.

Chromium oxide produces a superior sound found in high quality recording tapes. We are to record and playback the words of God with quality, no detractions and no distortion. Selenium trace amounts of selenium in the diet can actually protect humans against cancer and heart disease. It is the active element of vitamin G.

Phosphorus is essential to life; 20 percent of the human skeleton is made up of calcium phosphate. It is also a compound of DNA, and it boosts the cleaning efficiency of detergents.

Additional minerals:

Nickel is used in electrodes in batteries which make the battery rechargeable. (We can always recharge ourselves in the blood of Jesus, because the source never runs out.) Jesus paid the price for our salvation, recharging us with the Hoy Spirit. Cobalt trace elements are essential to human nutrition. This is present in meat and dairy products and Vitamin B-12. What it says here is our meat and dairy contain vitamins, and if natural meat contains nutrients for us, how much more does our nutrients come from the meat of the Word of God through His son Jesus.

Molybdenum is useful in medicine for producing images of the body to see the workings of the internal organs. The Bible says we are made in His image, so what's found in the blood produces an image of who we are.

Lithium carbonate has been used to treat patients with the severe mental illness known as bipolar disorder. We must not be double minded.

Boron combined with oxygen, water, and sodium forms a compound called borax, which is a cleaning agent. We can see why it is important to believe and accept the incorruptible blood of Jesus as our cleaning agent. When we believe in Jesus, this put us in a healing acceleration process of cleaning of our blood. There is only one diet that works for our total health, and that is the Lord's diet. All the elements of the blood do different things, if we accept the blood only halfway that would be accepting the blood but not activating the power of it in our life. Do we understand all that has been given to us? You can see that the effects will be big, when we don't accept the elements of power that the Holy Spirit has for our health.

[5]"Blood doesn't just lie motionless in the body. Sometimes when a person is badly cut, the blood seems to spurt out What's more, the spurting is in time with the beating of the heart, so people got the notion that the heart must squeeze and push blood out of itself, over and over again."

Everyone's heart beats you can feel your own heartbeat if you place your hand on your chest The heart beats regularly, about seventy times a minute in grown-ups and a little faster in children. The heart beats as long as you live, and when it stops, you die. Our heart moves more of the blood of salvation when we exercise it with the good news of the Bible. It's not just blood that's important to life, but also the movement of blood. We also see that we need to have purified blood, and it must be moving on our behalf for living a clean life. When God sent His Son as a messenger, He activated a movement with the blood to prepare our bodies to receive the Holy Spirit. Jesus will come into our container just the way it is, Jesus is no respecter of people, but he would like us to participate in the effort. Jesus moved the blood from his body to be poured out and into ours. We must think of all the activities of Jesus's blood which include pours, sheds, spattered, finds, pursues, fells, stained, rest, remembers, it vindicates for us, remains, heals, and regulates body heat. The blood activates healing to all areas of our life. Satan knows this creative spiritual force of the Lord since Satan was Lucifer once one of the archangels of the entire heavenly realm. He was God's right-hand man but only one had full power and authority over heaven and that was God. But Lucifer wanted to be the one with the power and authority. This resulted in him being cast out from heaven. He must have been very angry to be cast out of such a beautiful place as heaven. Lucifer, now called Satan, tries to create thoughts in our minds on how to operate,

---

[5]   Isaac Asimov, How Did We Find Out About Blood.

but there is only one producer of life, and there is only one that holds all the elements in his hands and that is God. The devil's spirit seeks a body to enter. The devil was an archangel at one time, but he is now a fallen angel and has no healing ability. Only God produces the blood of life with his words.

God assembled us and knows all the parts that He made us with. Before something is put into production to be sold (bought with a price) on the market, it has to have an instruction manual. The Bible is our manual for life, (Basic Instructions before Leaving Earth) and step-by-step instructions on how the product is assembled.

Something has to be made then taken apart in reverse order and numbered to know the part that goes together last before a manual can be written the production of the first item or sample must be made already (human beings). We are made in the image of God; we have to be part of the image to be in the image. The Bible says in the image, and (in) means in. The Bible says, "Taste and see that the Lord is good." Sample His life. He knows us all the way and even the very hairs of your head are numbered (Matt 10:30 KJV).

All the elements above points to what is in DNA (He was Dead, but Now, He is Alive). A hair analysis that is sent into a lab also reviews the makeup of different elements in our blood (our DNA). This is all part of production and service that makes us operate in the Kingdom of God. There must be a service center with 24-hour call line for service (that is the church) to answer any question about the assembling of a particular production item. If there is a part of the body that is not operating correctly, we must ask (in prayer) the Lord (the head service center operator) for instructions on how to make our bodies line up with the gospel. There is a trademark of ownership placed on us, but this is a trade secret and He doesn't want to let that secret be known to the wrong source because there can be no counterfeits. He holds the patent that patterns us after the Father, Son, and Holy Spirit. He holds the patent and key to the gates of hell. Satan and one third of the angels that fell will try to put parts inside of us that don't belong. God though has put His seal on us.

> "Set his seal of ownership on us, and put his Spirit in our hearts as a deposit, guaranteeing what is to come" (2 Cor 1:22 NIV).

God's spirit is in our heart, and He is in control of all the heart elements and intents that can be use. Remember earlier when I talked about the heart as the pump that keeps the blood flowing throughout the body. We must guard our fleshly heart as well as our spiritual heart. What does the Spiritual heart pump? The scripture says He deposited His Spirit in our hearts.

> "So will be our resurrection of the dead. The body that is sown is perishable, it is raised imperishable; it is sown in dishonor, it is raised in glory; it is sown in weakness; it is raised in power; it is sown in natural body, it is raised a Spiritual body" (1 Cor 15:44 NIV).

So it is written: "The first man Adam became a living being" The last Adam, a life-giving Spirit. The Spiritual did not come first, but the natural, and after that the Spirit (1 Cor 15:45 NIV).

God rescues us from death. As stated before, it is not enough to just have the blood, but it has to be moving and moving with Spiritual power. We need to take care of the natural body and watch what we put into our body. He wants our wine skin new before he pours in the new wine sent from heaven. The wine skin that the Bible is referring to is our fleshly body. We are to be ready when the Lord comes.

The Body of Healing Jesus

The Church is referred to as "The Body of Christ," "one body" (Rom. 12:4–5; 1 Cor. 10:17, 12:12–13, 20; Eph. 2:16, 4:4; Col. 3:15) "the body" (1 Cor. 12:14–16, 18, 19, 22–25; Eph. 4:16, 5:23), "the whole body" (1 Cor. 12:17; Eph. 4:16), "his body" (Eph. 1:23, 5:30), "same body" (Eph 3:6), "the body, the church" (Col. 1:24), "and all the body" (Col. 2:19).[1] Jesus died so that the body would be able to operate accordingly to the will of the Father, without sin. The body also doesn't operate without the blood, the purified blood; blood by itself without the body can't operate individually. Our earthly body is of a sinful nature inherent in Adam. The Holy Spirit conceived Jesus's body and our bodies were made from the dirt of the earth. Jesus's birth was the result of breaking blood from the virgin birth from the inside out Jesus looks at the insides of who we are and then the all-around health and intents of the heart. What heart? Is this our fleshly heart or spiritual heart? I truly believe that it is significant that he chose dirt to create man. The earth is made out of dirt, but the dirt was created by the spoken words that proceeded from the mouth of God. The earth is alive and the elements that are contained in it. If the earth was not alive, then the plants and trees would be dead. God said, "My word is spirit and life." God's word created the earth and

---

[1] Finis Jennings Dake, pg 518, God's Plan For Man, Lawrenceville Georgia, 1977.

called it good. To praise Him and cry out the earth has to be alive. To be green and bud there is life in the elements.

"Let the heaven and earth praise Him, the
seas and all that move in them" (Ps 69:32 NIV).

"I tell you, if they keep quiet, the stones will cry out" (Luke 19:40). It says the earth praise Him in one area and the stones cry out in another area.

He created man from something that He spoke into existence by His word and it says that, "It is good." Everything was created by the Word of God; no other word can create life but God's word. So as we use God's words and care for things, by the words that God created we are protecting and guarding creation. God did not send His son to condemn but to give life. God wanted children so He created a family unit, Adam and Eve. The dirt contained many living elements. He could have chosen any element around to create a body, being that all things where created by Him anyway. Dirt contained all the elements to create man and was here and in place already by Him. Remember, it is the spoken word that creates and that causes a reaction of the elements to create a body. We are just a small part of the overall body of Christ. The body of Adam was created and then the Holy Spirit was blown into it. The breath of life was alive with God even before it was blown into our body. The breath of life is described as a (Vital breath, Divine inspiration, Soul, and Spirit).[2] Adam received God's entire image, the Father, Son, and Holy Spirit. So how did sin come upon Him? Adam was deceived by the words of Eve, who was deceived by the words of the serpent, Satan. Adam's thought process was tricked into thinking that it was right, even though it was still Adam that made His own choice. The mind has blood flowing through it which continually washes and cleans it. We are cleansed also by the washing with water through the word. The word here is referred to as God's words for us that are documented in

---

[2] James Strong, Strong's Concordance Of The Bible, #5397, Publisher Thomas Nelson 1995.

the Bible. We see here the healing through the cleaning of blood and water. Jesus's heart poured out blood then water on the cross when He was pierced for us. This is Jesus's love for us, for the sins to be washed away for total family healing.

> "Husbands, love your wife, just as Christ loved the church and gave himself up for her to make her holy, cleansing her by the washing with water through the word" (Eph. 25–26 NIV).

What did we inherit from Adam? Adam received all the image of God, only now there was sin upon him also, this sin brought on the choice of right and wrong. We inherited it all, but we need to learn how to remove the sin part that was inherited from Adam's body. We can see when we use the word of God that it brings cleansing to make us Holy. Adam was saturated with sin that flowed through Him. If we are part of the body of Christ and the Spirit is in us when we believe, then it is time for the healing of our temple to take place. Then we can pray in tongues that will edify ourselves. Have you received the Holy Spirit since you believed? This brings on total communication with the Lord for fellowship.

> "This day I call heaven and earth as witnesses against you that I have set before you life and death, blessing and curse. Now choose life so that you and your children will live" (Dt 30:19 NIV).

The healing of doctors who are on earth is good, but there is the greatest physician of all times who set all the healing and medical rules in place to be used in the heart of His people. People's hearts stop in operating rooms all the time, and then they are brought back to life. What is being said? No, not just our earthly body is affected if we have made Jesus the Lord of our life. God means our spiritual eternal life with Him until eternity. The breath from God that gives life is referred to as CPR. The most important things to look for when an emergency medical technician (EMT) comes upon a scene of an accident are referred to as the ABCs.[3] A=Airway. God created our airway. B=Breathing, Christ offers us life using CPR. We can say the letters CPR also stands for Christ's Personal Restoration. Giving breath into our airway causes C=Circulation. God made sure that the breath given was circulating through our body to give us life. God wants us to circulate Spiritual life throughout the Church and to those who are lost. God was the first one to do this, and all medical responders still use CPR to save lives today.

God also blew His words inside us, but we have to learn the proper use. What have you done with the words God blew inside you since the time of your birth? "In the beginning was the word, and the word was with God, and the word was God" (1 John 1:1). "The spirit gives life; the flesh counts for nothing. The words I have spoken to you are Spirit and they are life" (John 6:63 NIV).

We are made in His image which includes his words that are Spirit and they are life. Life was in the beginning and was the word. There was one person that the Spirit was blown into and the benefits of all that went along with it were activated on down to us and that was Adam. We are descendants of Adam after he sinned. Ever since creation, the Spirit of the Word has been alive. But a spiritual separation happened; Adam chose to not operate with Spiritual power that existed with him. God said, "I'll never leave you nor forsake you." This is why we need the blood of Jesus to also heal the land because the environment around Adam and in Adam changed. Our environment on earth and the words being used around us are not the same environment and words that God wants us as Christians to use. We have been exposed to the world's words of deceit and unbelief to long. The Holy Spirit's words have been put aside. Through Jesus's death, we now have His Spiritual power deposited within us. We can say that the battery (Spirit) has been deposited inside us; Jesus doesn't want us to just sit the Spiritual power within us on a shelf somewhere and the shelf life or health and propriety run down. Our battery (Spirit) is to be used for the Kingdom of God. When we don't

---

[3]   Brady, First Responder Medical Guide, Sixth Edition, Prentice Hall, 2001.

give God the glory, we are in turn giving it to Satan and saying God doesn't have healing power. When we allow Satan to pull from our battery (Spirit), it is then being used by Satan to obtain His power. Satan has no power of His own that is why He hooks up his jumper cable to us. This gives Him power so he can steal, kill, and destroy in all areas of our life. This is why we need our jumper cables to be hooked up to the blood and healing power generator. Our generator of life will regenerate our lowered power and keep us fully charged to the top. We are to be prepared for those that are in need of a boost of healing energy and will want to hook up their jumper cables to us for power to boost them up. Jesus is a never-ending source of power and will never run empty. Finding fullness is found in the Bible that is full of the power of the Holy Spirit. He prepares a table to feed us in the mist of our enemies. God is saying "come home" and feast on the healing bread and wine.

When one brings the Holy Spirit into their heart earlier on in their lives, the benefit of doing so will reflect on their health the rest of their life from that point on. God's table is full of health and healing, so let us fill our plates and partake in His goodness. God doesn't want us to wait until we get to heaven to enjoy all the health benefits that go with what God's plan is for us now. God's son Jesus was alive spiritually before a body was provided for His Spirit to enter into, just as we were alive with Him spiritually before we were born physically, we were planned out in advance. One needs to understand the body as it pertains to the whole church, our part of the body of Christ, and yet still be their own individual self. We are only one blood vessel, which should connect to the next one and keep the blood flow of the power transferring throughout the whole church.

> "In him we were also chosen, having been predestined according to the plan of him who works out everything in conformity with the purpose of his will" (Eph 1:11 NIV).

If we have been chosen by Him and predestined ahead of time, then what are we worrying about? The plan has already been established for our life. The body must maintain its power and blood by exercising good health and spiritual practices. Both foods are to be eaten, body nutrient and spiritual nutrient, but only one will leave you hungering again. This is the fullness of what was spoken by God's word that we should eat and not hunger again. When we ask God to come into our heart, then we receive all He has to offer. The power is in the blood along with the Holy Spirit. We are cleansed of sin and now are as white as snow by the blood of Jesus.

> "Come close to God and he will come close to you. (Recognize that you are sinners, get your soiled hands clean; (realize that you have been disloyal) wavering individuals with divided interests, and purify your hearts (of your spiritual adultery)" (James 4:8 NIV).

One would ask, "If Jesus died over two thousand years ago for me and I'm only fifty-nine years old, how is that possible?" He died for my spirit by the cleaning away of my sins, pains, and iniquities. Our body belongs to God, but it is still its own individual spiritual part of the Holy Body. All parts of the Holy Body are just as important as the other parts. Our Creator was thinking of us long before a body was made. He gave us His armor before we needed it. He said, "I knew you before you were formed in your mother's womb." He said, "I knew you before you were fleshly formed." When we are at church and are in the sanctuary as we see people coming in the door, we can think of all the different members of Christ's body and say, "There's an arm, there's a foot, there's the kidneys, there's the heart, etc." All the parts assemble together and make up the body of Christ. This is the church (the people) that assembles with other members to form the body of believers or the body of Christ, just as different nations and nationalities are to assemble on earth for one common purpose, partaking in the blood of Jesus. The church is the bride, and I don't think that He was talking about a building here, but rather all the parts of His body.

"The body is a unit, though it is made up of many parts; and though all its parts are many, they form one body. So it is with Christ For we were all baptized by one Spirit into one body-whether Jews or Greeks, slave or free-and we were all given the one Spirit to drink" (1 Cor, 12–13 Thompson Chain-Reference Bible, NIV).

We are to stay healthy built up with the good words of the Bible. This will not only keep our flesh healthy but also the church that we attend. Before we can help other members of the body, we must make sure that we are strong enough to relay the power of healing words of what the blood has done for us and convey that to others in the neighborhood. If I'm part of the arm and I'm not operating with good health, then this blood will hinder the hand part of His body. When we hear and see other members of the body in need of healing, prayer, help in finances, maybe in need of a lift somewhere in a car or just a smile, then as a member of the body, we are to help that area that is not functioning the right way. We need to help it operate as the body of Christ with unstained blood flowing through and not being filled with sinful blood. We need to tell them all about the Blood of Jesus that heals all areas of our lives. Satan doesn't want us strong in Christ but under his control. When sin attacks the body with sickness and disease, it's like an anti-clotting substance.[4] "Some substances can prevent or slow down the formation of the blood clot Another group of substances called thrombolytic can make a fairly fresh blood clot loosen and disintegrate. They are often used as clot-busting agents." Satan acts as a clot buster, and he wants us to remain unhealed and weak. God created the body to heal itself with the protection of the Spirit around it, but when we remain in fellowship with him, we receive supernatural healing within our inner man. The protection that is around us now lives in us. God is the potter and we are the clay, God molded us in his image, but if enough sickness, disease, and other body-harming substances were to attack us

---

4   Steve Parker, Look at your body, pg 8.

all at once this would overwhelm our body system when it is without God's protection of the blood of Jesus. That's why we are dependent on all the other parts, for example, the older men should teach the younger men and older women teach the younger women. The Word is to be passed on as an inheritance to our children's children. Then there is Satan that wants to see to it that this process is stopped. That is what Satan is doing, overwhelming us with junk that causes life's disorders. If we let Satan have His chance to break down our body, our Spirit container is affected and that affects the blood health as a disease.

"Anemia is defined as a decrease in either hemoglobin or the number of red blood cells that are below the normal level. Iron is an essential ingredient in hemoglobin. If you do not have enough iron in your body, you cannot make enough hemoglobin. This form of anemia is called iron-deficiency anemia. Iron is an essential component of hemoglobin, which is the protein in red blood cells. Insufficient iron in your body causes an inadequate production of hemoglobin, and therefore leads to iron-deficiency anemia. The anemia of chronic disease frequently complicates other diseases. Disorders that often bring on this type of anemia include rheumatoid arthritis, hepatitis and tuberculosis. It can also occur in anyone who has as acute infection such as pneumonia. Red blood cell production takes place in the bone morrow, and depends substantially on two vitamins, vitamin B12 and folic acid. Your body absorbs these vitamins from certain foods. If you do not get enough of either vitamin, then the red blood cells that are formed are defective. The result is one of these forms of anemia. In North America nearly everyone's diet contains sufficient quantities of B12. A deficiency of the vitamin usually occurs because your body cannot absorb it. In a healthy person, the liver contains reserves of vitamin B12. If you develop an inability to absorb B12 your body will eventually deplete these reserves and anemia will develop."[5] The vitamins I like to take are vitamin G, vitamin O, and vitamin D (God's vitamins, the Word) and have a sufficient quantity

---

[5]   American Medical Association, Family Medical Guide, blood disorders, pg 426. Publisher Random House, 1990.

on hand to store within my heart and never run out. God refills our prescription for us day and night. Satan wants to steal them from you.

> "The thief comes only to steal kill and destroy; I have come that they may have life, and have it to the full" John 10:10 NIV).

It's a good thing we have a redeemer and He wants us full. If we are full of God's Spiritual vitamins, then there is no room for anything else and we are purged of ungodliness.

> "Until I come and take you to a land like your own land, of grain and new wine, land of bread and vineyards, land of olive trees and honey. Choose life and not death" (2 Kings 18:32 NIV).

One can live in good health all the days of one's life and not know Jesus as their Savior. But when healing needs to take place in our body, it is great to know for sure that we are going to be healed in a timely manner or in an instant by a miracle and also be healed of all our sinful ways so that heaven is the outcome. It's always in the Lord's best timing. People are continually studying how to stay in good health and eat right. Healing and health issues are solved best when one accepts Jesus as Lord.

> "Both the one who makes men holy and those who are made holy are of the same family" Hebrew 2:11 NIV).

We see that we have a process of choosing the things that we do and the things we feed on in our lifetime. Making sure that what we feed on are the proper nutrients for our blood. What we live and do and where we are in our life now is the result of choices we have made up to this point. A lifetime on earth is different than eternity with

God. When we accept Jesus as Lord, we start a process of experiencing heaven here on earth. His will is still going forward to be done on earth whether we get into the flow of his will or rebel against it Jesus went through death with His body so we wouldn't have to with ours.

"Thy kingdom come. Thy will be done in earth as it is in heaven" (Matt 6:14 KJV).

"Here I am, I have come to do your will." He sets aside the first to establish the second. "And by that will, we have been made holy through the sacrifice of the body of Jesus Christ once for all" (Hebrews 10:9–10 NIV).

Jesus wants His kingdom and will to be done on earth, "now." Jesus left a will, just as a person leaves a will and testament of his inheritance for his children. The blood of Jesus was willfully laid down so that the inheritance of the Father would still be moving. When He died, the will was read and distributed as it was written, but in the world, the IRS and government have their hands on the inheritance taxes and take their 65 percent share. This is why Jesus rose again to make sure that the full inheritance of the will went to His children. The blood of Jesus contains no sicknesses or diseases so we can have life and live healed. Being healed means more than the wholeness in our body and our health, it means healed in all areas of life: marriage, the relationship with one's parents, or land, but most of all the spiritual separation is gone and we are reconnecting with God. The spirit of darkness doesn't affect us any longer because we now walk in the light of God.

When people cut us with harsh words, it hurts; likewise when we are wounded or cut physically it hurts also. "As soon as the tissues are damaged and the blood leaks from the vessels, cells release chemicals that make the blood platelets sticky. These round or oval no nucleated disk clumps together to begin the clot. At the same time, strands of a substance called fibrin are formed. Millions of these strands form a netlike mesh that traps more blood cells. This clump of trapped cells forms the clot that plugs the wound. Gradually, the clot hardens into a scab, which protects the damaged tissue. Underneath, the ends of the wound grow together completing the healing process."[6] As we believe more and increase our relationship with Jesus, He keeps the healing process active. The Bible says we are healed by the blood of Jesus; it is His blood that heals us and not our own blood, when we eat the bread of life and drink the wine of Jesus's body. And according to the law almost all things are purified with blood, and without shedding of blood there is no remission (Heb 9:22 KJV).

Let's prove that the blood is alive for our healing; look at Gen 4:10.

The Lord said, "What have you done? Listen! Your brother's blood cries out to me from the ground. Now you are under a curse and driven from the ground, which opened its mouth and received your blood brother's blood from your hand, when you work the ground, it will no longer yield its crop for you. You will be a restless wanderer on the earth" (Gen 4:10–12 NIV).

It says that the blood cried out from the ground. Thank God for sending His Son to redeem us from the law and curses. "The Blood of Jesus has a voice and Hebrews 12:24 tell us that it speaks better things than the blood of Abel. The better things declared by Christ's blood are words of mercy, where as Abel's blood cried for vengeance. No matter what your needs may be the Blood of Jesus is speaking to God for mercy on our behalf."[7] Jesus is speaking because we tend to foul up too many things with our own words because we have the wrong intents in our heart. Man has been snared by his own word. It's the blood that allows us to talk the words that bring life. We are to use the words of life and good intents of our heart, not to be fooled by the deadly intents Satan has to trick us with. Just as the blood flows in our bodies, the words we learn about the blood must be flowing and not just bottled up inside us. There was love bottled up inside Jesus, and He let all the love become released by the blood

---

6 American Medical Association, Family Medical Guide, pg 427, Publisher Random House, 1990.

7 Marilyn Hickey, The Power of The Blood. Pg 22.

that poured out. There are lost sheep that need to be led to the right pasture, so the love of Jesus can be released to them. Jesus comes to minister to us by teaching, preaching, and healing us all. We are to bring in the lost and remind them that they are not to go one minute longer without knowing about Jesus and anything that they are going through has been paid for. For this is the greatest of all commissions.

When we stand in the gap for our brothers and sister, then the love that Jesus gave us is pouring out on them. I remember in high school, there was a big bully that was picking on this little boy named Joe just because he was bigger and couldn't fight back. I spoke up to the bully, knowing that I could hold my ground, and I said, "If you want someone to pick on, why don't you pick on someone your own size like me?" That was the last day that bully picked on that little boy. Wow, I felt great about standing in the gap because that day, that little boy was set free from the bully. There is a bully that has tried to take us out, but Jesus stood in and took all the pain for us, and suffering, scourging, and all the lashes that were for us. He made all the bullies of the world flee.

I remember at a young age before five years old, I was pushing a glider-type swing and I fell under it. It came down on my head, gashed it open, and it started to bleed. My father rushed home in the chief's fire car, and my father was quick to comfort me. If my earthly father came to comfort me like that, how much more will our Father God that sent His Son comfort and heal us? My father asked if I would like to ride in the fire car to the hospital, which got my mind off my injury. Jesus will cleanse our mind and thoughts with the blood and totally get our mind steered toward Him. I also remember that after my biological father died, when I was five years old, my mother told me that I'm the man of the house now. If only I knew all of what she was teaching me. I was the head of the household temporarily till my mother remarried when I was ten years old. When she remarried, I gave my stepfather the honor and respect of calling him Dad from the first time I met him because he was taking care of us and later adopted me into his family. That day, my earthly name changed. When we accepted Jesus into our heart and confess Him as Lord over our life and believe that He shed His blood for us, then there is a heavenly name change. When we are adopted by Jesus into God's family, we are to give Him all of our respect and reverence, for He changed our name from "Sinner" to "Child of God." All of that in His will is for our inheritance. When I go to work day after day, I ask myself if what I'm doing with my hands at work is going to leave an inheritance to my children's children. Is it possible that the houses or a place I helped build or work will someday belong to my children's children? I say yes. Better yet if I can tell my children about the wonderful healing over my life from where I was to where I'm going to be later and that is with the Father in heaven, then and only then have I done what I was called to do. When the family curse of unbelief is lifted to you Father God and all hurts, pains, and past events are all released, and then Father God's family will be healed. The greatest inheritance that comes from the Father is the Words of the Bible and that they are truth and all the events really did happen for our behalf. It is good to know that there will be a new heaven and a new earth and that we will receive a new body. We are now part of the overall body of Christ, the bride that He will receive, this bride (the church) will be white and pure as a virgin without sin. How many people are still not tapping into the goodness of Jesus? When one looks around at all of the created things from God that is in front of them, how can they believe that they are not included also as part of the overall blessings? The Bible has been written and will never change what is said about what Jesus did for our healing and peace of mind.

I'm have been crucified with Christ and I no longer live, but Christ lives in me.

> "The life I live in the body, I live by faith in
> the Son of God, who loved me and gave himself
> for me" (Gal 2:20 NIV).

When we admit that it is unhealthy to live that way any longer and call out to Jesus to renew our live, we are saying, "Jesus, I love what you did for me, thank you." Everything our body does is being recorded in a book to be reviewed later in heaven. This book will be the book of life, if we believe in what Jesus did for us. When I came to the full understanding of the love poured out for me that day on the cross, it was the most wonderful felling of love that anyone could give. I soon realized that the love is not leaving and that I have it with me. Then just knowing that the power and authority has also been giving to me to use for His Glory for healing was great. I now know what this body of mine was made for and that is so God can do His works through me. God is using us to get the good news of the Gospel out to a dying world. Being saved knows that you are going to be forever with Him. We as believers will be called away to heaven with Jesus and will return with Jesus to the final battle, and then there will be a new heaven and a new earth. There will be no more death, sorrow, pain, or tears.

The Blood of Jesus
for Deliverance

All the plagues and judgments wrought by Moses had not set even one Israelite free, it was not until the Blood of the Lamb was shed that their deliverance was affected. So also is our deliverance through Christ when His blood was shed, that the bondage of sin was broken.

> "And hath made of one blood all nations of man for to dwell on all the free of the earth, and hath determined the times before appointed, and the bound of their habitations; That they should seek the Lord, If haply they might feel after him thought he be not far from every one of us" (Acts 17:26–28 NIV).

Even though the Lord is near to everyone, it is amazing how far someone can become separated from God through sin and no forgiveness toward others. People from different nations have different blood elements depending on nutrients in the dirt their food is grown in, but through the body of Jesus, we are one blood. Each one of us must know the part we play in life to further help the kingdom of God. We see rebellion against the body of Christ everywhere, but there is only one blood that hath made all nations. "For the word of God is living and active. Sharper than any double-edge sword. It penetrates even to the dividing soul and spirit, joints and marrow; it judges the thoughts and attitudes of the heart" (Hebrews 4:12 NIV).

We see that words being used wrong will deactivate the healing process. We also know that the words of God are living and active, the blood is alive through penetration and dividing of the soul and the Spirit, joints and marrow. So because of oneself in their sins, we can't put the blame on anything but ourselves. But Jesus took the blame for us, so we didn't have to be as dead bones lying in waste.

> "The hand of the Lord was upon me, and he brought me out by the Spirit of the Lord and set me in the middle of a valley; it was full of bones on the floor of the valley, bones that were very dry. He asked me, 'Son of man, can these bones live?' I said, 'O Sovereign Lord, you alone know.' Then he said to me, 'Prophesy to these bones and say to them. Dry bones, here the word of the Lord!'
>
> "This is what the sovereign Lord says to these bones: 'I will make breath enter you, and you will come to life. I will attach tendons to you and make flesh come upon you and cover you with skin; I will put breath in you, and you and cover you with skin, I will put breath in you, and you will come to life. Then you will know that I am the Lord'" (Ezekiel 37:1–6 Thompson Chain Reference Bible).

"The Lord said, 'He will make breath enter in, attach tendons, make flesh and it will come to life, and then you will know that I'm the Lord. He is the creator of all life; the Lord had delivered us from our trespasses. They overcome him by the blood of the Lamb and by the word of their testimony'" (Rev 12:11 NIV). He activated the blood cell creation in the bone marrow.[1] "In your lifetime, you'll lose about 600 bones! As stated earlier, before you were born, your skeleton contained over 800 separate bones, many of which grew or fused together so that you had about 450 at birth by age 20, when

---

[1] The bone and skeleton book, Stephen Cumbaa.

your bones have finished growing and the separate parts have joined together, they'll number only 206." Look at Hebrews 4:12 where it says God's word is living and active penetrating and dividing joints and marrow. God's word is getting into your marrow and becoming active when you become a believer in Him and what He did for us on the cross. God's word is the same yesterday, today, and tomorrow. The Bible says that we are jointed with God, joined to His family bone to bone. He wants us to realize that we are joined to Him in all areas of our life, Body, Soul, and Spirit. Not only are we jointed bone to bone, but also flesh to flesh.

> "So the Lord God caused the man to fall into a deep sleep. And while he was sleeping he took one of the man's ribs and closed up the place with flesh. Then the Lord God made a woman from the rib he had taken out of the man, and he brought her to the man. The man said, 'This is now bone of my bone s and flesh of my flesh; she shall be called woman, for she was taken out of man'" (Gen 2:21–23 NIV).

[2]"Joints in reference to the body permit movement, but also give under sudden pressure to absorb potential shocks to the body." We are also joined to Him with our thought process and feelings and He absorbs our shock for us. Spiritually, we are joined by the new birth of the Spirit with power when we receive Jesus into our heart Jesus took the shock and pressure of our bodies away on the cross, not the devil. [3]The body is made up of two types of blood cells; the two types are red blood cells and white blood cells. The red blood cells contain a protein called hemoglobin, which combines with oxygen and releases it to the tissues as the blood circulates throughout our body. The red blood cells also carry the waste product carbon dioxide from the tissues to the lungs, so hemoglobin, which combines with oxy-

---

[2] The bone and skeleton book, Stephen Cumbaa.
[3] American Medical Association.

gen, our body also contains white blood cells that protect the body from different infections. There are several different kinds of white blood cells, most of them are neutrophils, which attack and engulf bacteria. Another kind of white blood cell is a lymphocyte, which recognizes foreign cells, infectious agents, and other foreign substances and participates in the body's immune reaction against them. [4]In the inherited disease called sickle-cell anemia, the red blood cells contain abnormal hemoglobin, called hemoglobin S. If you have this disease, you have no normal hemoglobin in your red cells because you have inherited a sickle-cell gene from each of your parents. Thaiassemia is another disease in which an inherited defect prevents the formation of normal amounts of hemoglobin A, the type of hemoglobin that is found in the red blood cells after the first few months of life. Hemolytic anemia is a disorder in which your red cells are destroyed prematurely. When this occurs, your body attempts to compensate by producing new red cells at a faster rate. If destruction exceeds production, the resulting disorder is called hemolytic anemia. Hemolytic anemia may be hereditary.

In which case, it is present at birth or soon afterward, or you may acquire it later in life.

In the references mentioned, you have probably noticed that the word *hereditary* was used. Jesus came to break any generational curses that may be put on us from our family members sins from times past. We are in a sin environment in this world, but the Bible says we are not of this world. More and more, we are seeing the importance of the blood and trying to keep the cells healthy and in balance, free of sin.

> "He who feeds on my flesh and drinks my blood has eternal life, and I will raise him up on the last day. For my fresh is true and genuine food, and my blood is true and genuine drink. He who feeds on My blood dwells continually in Me, and I in him" (John 6:54–56).

---

[4] Family medical guide, pg 429–430.

Jesus is in us when we continually feed on His blood and drinks of His blood. Jesus blood covered all areas that he would next enter, which was beneath the earth; he entered into Hades (hell). First Jesus covered the earth with his healing power of the blood before he entered the area that is known as Hades, which contained sin. Sin is the thing that our body was not designed for, but we let sin in through the choices we have made. While on the tree (or cross) first the blood poured out of Jesus and then the water, "blood cells are carried by watery, salty fluid called plasma."[5] Plasma helps total cleansing of our bodies by carrying the blood cells through our soul. The first breath we took is the one that God blew into man. At that time, He also blew into us His Word. "In the beginning was the Word, and the Word was with God, and the Word was God" (John 1:1 KJV).

The word was God and God blew inside us what was contained within Him. What have you done with the words that the Lord blew into you at birth? Have you used them to build up people or to tear them down? The words we use will be effective one way or the other, to activate life or to bring death and separation. In the beginning while in the Garden of Eden, God said, "Of all the trees in the garden there is one that you are forbidden to eat from, the tree of the knowledge of good and evil, or you will surely die." Now the serpent deceived Eve, the serpent said you would not die. In the garden, Eve offered Adam a dying fruit because she removed the forbidden fruit from the tree's vine or life source. There was a separation of nutrition (blood of the plant life) all elements that were feeding the fruit, there was no longer production of life (chlorophyll) flowing through the fruit Just as the blood of a grape is the juice, Jesus's blood is referred to as the fruit of the vine. The Bible says the wages of sin is death. There was sin because there was a disconnection as a result of sin and disobedience.

Sin brings on sickness and diseases of the body that are set in every possible organ including mental, and emotional, and spiritual diseases. Sin also came on the land and polluted it. This was a paradise made perfect and with purity, without corruption from outside

---

5   Bergeron, Biziak, and, Brady First Responder sixth edition.

influences and sin came on man then spread throughout the land. While we remained connected to God through Jesus, there is life flowing through us. That is why we need to remain connected to God for our life source. If our bodies lack in nutrition, then a vitamin substitute is often the place we turn. Just a while ago, I mentioned chlorophyll, there is a health product called.[6] "Chlorophyll, which is a blood builder, a digestive tract detoxifier, supports intestinal health, supports circulatory health and just happens to be the blood of plant life." Remember the Bible says life is in the blood. The Bible also says that "Jesus was hung on a tree." It also says Jesus is the branch. Jesus chose to lay His life down on the tree so that the life source and the knowledge were restored, Jesus had the power to fight off any one that tried to nail Him to the cross, but He chose not to for our sake. Do you really think Jesus needed the nails to hold Him to the cross?

Jesus will continually regenerate blood cells so they will be flowing to us because Jesus was raised from the dead. He removed sin from us like one flushes out a car radiator until it is clear, clean, and white as snow. Jesus will continually stand in the gap for us. We do not have the ability to attach ourselves to the tree and reestablish the life source to it because we were exposed to death or sin. Our blood has been weakened and tainted by sin from a foreign substance that doesn't belong in the body. There are four ways the body takes on foreign substances: ingestion, injection, absorption, inhalation. One can also say that foreign substances enter into our thought process.

God blow into us the life source from the environment He has been living in.

> "Then the Lord God formed man from the dust of the ground and breathed into his nostrils the breath or spirit of life and man became a living being" (Genesis 2:7).

When God formed woman while the man was in a deep sleep, He removed a rib. The rib bone is one of the bones of the body that

---

6   Nature's Sunshine product INC.

has the most bone marrow. The rib bone also contained blood cells (DNA) from the side of man; this left a weak spot in the side of man. The woman is known as the weaker vessel. The devil had to attack the woman to find the weak spot of the man, and that was the woman who was formed from the rib of man. The ribs are the protective cage area that protects the inner parts of our body where Satan wants to attack. The innermost parts are the blood flowing and waste-removing areas, mainly the heart of man.

Let's talk about reproduction of human life. While in the womb, the baby receives nutrients and oxygen from the mother's blood. At birth, the delivery is watched closely to make sure that the head of the baby does not pinch off the umbilical cord. The source of the breath of life is within the blood. Remember, the breath of life from Father God activated the blood and got it moving within Adam.) Also, in women reproduction, a woman produces eggs as part of a monthly process called the menstrual cycle, which begins at puberty. During the menstrual cycle, the female reproductive system undergoes a series of changes that prepare it for fertilization and pregnancy. If the egg is not fertilized, a shedding of blood is associated with this process. This is a cleansing time of unfertile eggs. This is our fleshly being, but who fertilizes our Spiritual reproduction?

The blood of Jesus does if we let Him reproduce the love He has for us. "And suddenly, a woman who had a flow of blood twelve years came from behind and touched the hem of His garment For she said to herself, 'If only I may touch His garment I shall be made well.' But Jesus turned around, and when He saw her He said, 'Be of good cheer, daughter; your faith has made you well.' And the women was made well from that hour" (Matt 9:20–22, KJV).

Don't you know that there was twelve years of cleansing of the blood; there must have been a replacement of old blood cells for new ones. There was a continual flow of blood, for if this blood flowed for so long without replenishing, she would have died. She knew where the source of healing was and that was to get to the hem of Jesus. As soon as she touched Jesus, her heart started the reproduction of healing in her body. Because of her faith, and being in the presence of Jesus, His words activated a process of remembrance of what He did for her. Do you not see and know that your bodies are members (bodily parts) of Christ (the Messiah) (1 Corinthians 6:15).

Just knowing that our bodies are part of the makeup of Christ should make us shout for joy! Repeat that sounding joy with every heart beat.

> "Do you not know that your body is the temple (the very sanctuary) of the Holy Spirit who is in you, whom you have received from God?" 1 Corinthians 6:19).

We are to praise him in the sanctuary, which is from the very center of our being the heart, soul, and spirit. He is the one who gave us our heart which serves as a pump for the blood. Let us give the Father the proper thanks for all He has done for us.

Besides pumping blood, these are some of the other inherited heart activities:

Set. My Son Shechen has his heart set on your daughter (Gen 34:8 NIV).

Prompts. Man whose heart prompts him to give (Ex 25:2 NIV).

Moved. Everyone who was willing and whose heart moved him came and brought an offering (Ex 35:21 NIV).

Turns, Make sure that there is no man or woman, clan or tribe among you today whose heart turns away from the Lord (Dt 29:18 NIV).

Rejoices. My heart rejoices in the Lord (1 Sa 2:1 NIV).

Feared. Feared for the ark of the Lord (1 Sa 4:13 NIV).

Failed. His heart failed him and he became as a stone (1 Sa 25:37 NIV).

Desires. That you may rule over all your heart's desire (2 Sa 3:21 NIV).

Longed. King's heart longed for Absalom (2 Sa 14:1 NIV).

Carried. Why has your heart carried you away and why do your eyes flash, so that you vent your rage against God and pour out such words from your mouth? (Job 15:12 NIV).

Rages. A man's own folly ruins his life, yet his heart rages against the Lord (Pr 19:3 NIV).

Instructs. Even at night my heart instructs me (Ps 16:7 NIV).

Leaps, my heart leaps for joy and I will give thanks to Him in song (Ps 28:7 NIV).

Trembles. My heart trembles at your word.

Yearns. My heart yearns within me (Job 19:27 NIV).

Sings. the widow's heart sings (Job 29:13).

Pounds. At this my heart pounds and leaps from it place (Job 37:1 NIV).

Harbors. The godless in heart harbors resentment (Job 36:13).

Gathers. Whenever one comes to see me, he speaks falsely, while his heart gathers slander, then he goes out and spreads it aboard (Ps 41:6 NIV).

Grows. My heart grows hot within me (Ps 39:3 NIV).

Praise. Let all the upright in heart praise him (Ps 64:10 NIV).

Fails. My heart fails within me (Ps 40:12 NIV).

Loves. I will get up now and go about the city, through it streets and squares; I will search for the one my heart loves (SS 3:2 NIV).

Sank. My heart sank at his departure (SS 5:5 NIV).

Afflicted. His heart was afflicted for us cries. Holy, Holy, Holy with the thought of a Guide. A wise man's heart guides his mouth, and his lips promote instruction (Pr 16:32 NIV).

Trust. The Lord is my strength and shield; my heart trusts in Him and I'm helped.

Heart. Is like medicine (Pr 17:22 NIV).

Blameless. I will walk in my house with blameless heart (Ps 101:2 NIV).

We have been exposed to the sinfulness of the world for so long that some think that this is the normal way to life. We can see that when the blood was poured out for us, all the activities also went with it and so much more. In our hearts, Jesus had to show us how to let our feelings that had been suppressed do to all the sin nature around us. By letting out feelings of love toward our fellow man and letting the inner healing of man take place. The heart activity has to be in God's timing with the purified blood flow of Jesus, which is where we get our deliverance. The blood of Jesus removes the sinful intents of the heart. Emotions were released, burdens where removed, and yokes broken as the heart feelings started to flow again. Jesus can never return the blood; it has been delivered to all who chose to believe and be cleared of all that is bottled up inside them as bad blood intentions and actions. He came to set us free, and if the Son sets you free, you are free indeed. We are only free to do what was originally planned and ordained by God. Why does it take so much to bring the feelings and emotions out of his people again? Jesus wants us to be a part of the process also, make the decision today to follow Jesus. Does one get so far into sin that they are immune to the effects of sin? Yes, Satan is a good counterfeiter. We must remember that Satan is only a counterfeiter and does not have the real stuff to get us anywhere in life. Have you received the Holy Spirit since you have believed? There is a language between you and God and that is the Holy Spirit with tongues of power. We need to receive our prayer language of tongues to edify ourselves.

> "For any one that speaks in a tongue does not speak to men but to God. Indeed no one understands him; he utter mysteries with his spirit" (1 Co 14:2 NIV).

There is a time when Jesus has to go to the Father for our behalf, but he left us knowing by saying, "And if I go prepare a place for you, I will come back and take you to be with me that you also may be where I am. You know the place where I am going." We not only been delivered from sin, but Jesus also gave us knowledge of the place where He is going, and that is to visit for a short time with His Father in heaven. While Jesus was there, He received his Father's full power to bring back to us. Jesus said, "You heard me say. 'I am going away and I will come back to you.' If you love me, you would be glad that I'm going to the Father, for the Father is greater than I" (John 14:28 NIV).

Apart from Jesus, you can do nothing, for He is our deliverer. He delivers us first class. We can fight against Satan because we have been endowed with power from on high.

Healing Blood
of Jesus

First, let us understand our need for healing, what is it that needs healing in our life, our body, soul, land, and to regain a connection with the Spirit? In the Garden of Eden, "God said that you shall not eat of the tree of the knowledge of good and evil, blessing and calamity" (Gen 2:17 KJV). So are we in need of healing here after the forbidden fruit was removed and eaten? Yes, I would say, but what kind of healing? Adam and Eve saw themselves naked in the Garden. What was it that was removed from them? The spiritual covering of the Holy Spirit was not covering them anymore. The Holy Spirit was there only they decided to operate without its covering, do things on their own. Our body didn't die at this point, but God said there would be death.

And the Lord God commanded man, "You are free to eat from any tree in the Garden; but you shall not eat of the tree of the knowledge of good and evil, for when you eat of it you will surely die" (Gen 2:16–17 NIV).

This was a spiritual death or separation from God. The protection of the Spirit was not present with them, a choice was made on whom to listen to, and it was the deceiver that got their ear and not the thoughts of what God said. We must look beyond ourselves and what God set up for our life way beforehand. Understanding God's plan for us has always been a struggle in the heart of His children. God set us up in paradise, a place of no sin or death, a place where no death had to happen to pay for sins because sin was not present yet. Everything we needed was provided to us in the garden, but man wanted more and to do his own thing. We always want to mess up a good thing, you've heard the saying, "If it wasn't broken to start with, don't try to fix it."

> "If my people, who are called by my name, shall humble themselves, pray, seek, crave, and required of necessity my face and turn from their wicked ways, then will I hear from heaven, forgive their sin, and heal their land" (2 Chr 7:14 KJV).

It says that he will heal their land, what happened to the land? Sin came upon the land. We are called by His name, and the sheep have to recognize His voice for the healing to take place. The sheep that know Him will recognize His voice. "For many are called, but few are chosen" (Matt 22:14 KJV).

He is calling all sinners to recognize what the shed blood has done for them. We see here that there are different types of healing for our physical being and also the land in which we live. God want us to be in a Garden of Eden again the way he created it to be. There is healing of the physical body from sin, and there is healing of the land. Jesus covered the earth with His protection (His blood shed and fell on the earth); the earth that Adam first knew was called the Garden of Eden. There was nothing wrong with the land in the Garden, until sin was able to have an open door and come upon the land. We are to leave an inheritance for our children's children. We are to teach our children about the Blood of Jesus that healed us and can heal our land that we live. Look at the inheritance that our Father God left for us. The healing over our family comes from living the life that God has for us and being an example unto our children and also to pass on the knowledge we learn from the Word of God. Once we achieve knowledge, we are not to keep it to ourselves but to share it with nonbelievers and other members of His body. This is where the healing is passed along through the body.

"But unto you who revere and worshipfully fear My name shall the Son of Righteousness arise with healing in His wings and His beams, and you shall go forth and gambol like calves (released) from the stall and leap for joy" (Malachi 4:2 AMP).

When we are faced with what seems to be overwhelming odds of hardships in life, such as the feeling that one is faced with in the waiting room of a hospital, while our loved one are in the hands of the doctors, their blood and body are in the hands of the doctor, there is worry, sadness, hope, and expectancy of what is going to happen to our loved ones. Let us look at the end of Malachi 4:2; it says there is leaping for joy because of the process of being set free from what has been ailing them or holding them back. It is expected that the doctors studied the human body and is knowledgeable about the working of it. But in our time of healing, who better to run to than the one that created us, the Father? There is none other than God, but we must go through the Son to get to the Father. God gave even the doctors the wisdom to heal through the laying on of hands as they operate, if they are a believer and operating with the power of the Holy Spirit, they are operating hand to hand with God as their guide. Remember doctors operate on us according to our faith in the healing process of the blood of Jesus. Back in the Garden of Eden, death came on the land after the forbidden fruit was removed from the vine and eaten by Adam.

There was a disconnection of the fruit by Eve from the vine or branch in the Garden of Eden. Jesus is labeled as the branch in the Bible. It even says that He will prune of any branches that don't bear fruit. If we are walking where death is or on polluted land, don't you think it would start to try to get on us or absorb into our bodies? If we are healed but are still walking on polluted ground, then there needs to also be a healing on the land. Before one accepts the Lord as their savior and protector, one would be lost and unprotected from the environment that surrounds them. Jesus is with you to give you

His full protection. Jesus gives us weapons and armor to use and we don't use them.

"Yes, though I walk through the (deep, sunless) valley of the shadow of death, I will fear or dread no evil, for You are with me; Your rod (to protect) and Your staff (to guide), they comfort me" (Psalm 22:4 AMP). Psalms 22:4 Amp says it is a shadow of death, not death, only a shadow.

We must believe that Jesus was sent to die for us and rose again for our sins to be removed and accept the truth that He is Lord by confession and taking Him into our hearts as our Lord and savior. Take Him into our hearts (the place our blood is pumped). Jesus is auditing every blood cell as it enters and exits the heart of man, is it filling with intents or washed clean. Jesus is our protector and healer when we walk through the valleys that have shadows of death. It says that He is with us and guiding us. Remember that we are only passing through the valley and not stopping to camp out there.

> "Jesus answered, 'I assure you, most solemnly I tell you unless a man is born of the water and the Spirit, he cannot enter the kingdom of God. What is born of (from) the flesh is flesh (of the physical is physical); what is born of the Spirit is Spirit'" (John 3:5–6 AMP).

It says born of the Spirit. The Spirit is alive. This is a three-part process, our flesh, the Spirit within, and also the land we live. Jesus went through the land, clearing sin.

Jesus went throughout Galilee, teaching in their synagogues, preaching the good news of the kingdom, and healing every disease and sickness among the people. News about Him spread all over Syria, and people brought to him all who were ill with various diseases, those suffering severe pain, the demon possessed, those having seizures, and the paralyzed and he healed them. Large crowds from Galilee, the Decapolis, Jerusalem, Judea, and the region across the Jordan followed him (Matt. 4:23 NIV, Thompson Chain Reference Bible).

It says Jesus was healing every disease and sickness among the people. It doesn't say healed first. At first, the healing word was spoken, the process continually took place as the words of Him started to spread, people had faith that a good thing was happening. People started to seek Him; it says people brought to Him all who were ill. After that, He healed them, large crowds followed Him. Through all this, it doesn't say they followed after the Devil who steals kills or destroys; as a matter fact, it says the demon-possessed were healed. Then the healing was across their land. The devil gets no credit for healing because he is not the one with the healing power that is in the blood that was poured out.

In the Old Testament, animal blood was accepted by God for a substitute for death (Ezek 18:20) which the sinner deserved: "For the life of the flesh is in the blood, and I have given it to you upon the altar to make atonement for your souls" Although Old Testament believers were truly forgiven and received genuine atonement through animal sacrifice. They are to take some of the blood and put it on the sides and tops of the doorframes of the houses where they eat the lambs (Ex 12:1 NIV).

The blood must be of year-old males without defect. Blood is alive, that means that we can put life protection upon our house. Our house is our body where we house the Holy Spirit. Where is the doorframe of your house? Where are you to put the blood? The door is our heart that lets in all of the Holy Spirit into our life. "The blood will be a sign for you on the houses where you are; and when I see the blood, I will pass over you. No destructive plague will touch you when I strike Egypt" (Ex 12:13 NIV).

Now when he sees the blood on the tops and sides of the doorframes, the Lord will Passover and not permit the destroyer to enter in and strike you down. What went on here is the belief in the power of the blood. The person had to hear about putting the blood on their doorframe from someone for their protection first of all. The Lord spoke to Moses and Aaron to tell the entire congregation about how to put blood on their doorframe for protection from the destroyer. Moses and Aaron were given direct instructions on what to say as they carried out those instructions. The congregation had to do their part by listening to the words spoken to them and acting on them. Don't just be a hearer but a doer of the word; this is what keeps us safe. The New Testament clearly states that during the Old Testament period. God's justice was not served: "For it is not possible that the blood of bulls and goats could take away the sins" (Heb 10:4).

Atonement was possible "because in His forbearance God had passed over the sin that were previously committed" (Rom 3:25). However, God's justice was served in the death of Jesus Christ as a substitute who "not with the blood of goats and calves, but with His own blood He entered the Holy Place once for all."[1] We must remember that He entered only once for all. Jesus was sent to save all in the world for He was perfect and without sin. Accepting the blood allows us to enter into the Holy Place where the Veil was rid.[2] The veil that separated God and us was the flesh. Now we also have liberty to enter the Holy place because of Jesus's blood. Sin kept us from our liberty, and we felt ashamed to try to approach God.

Surely, He borne our griefs (sicknesses, weaknesses, and distresses) and carried our sorrows and pains (of punishment), yet we (ignorantly) considered Him stricken smitten and afflicted by God (as if with leprosy). But He was wounded or our transgressions. He was bruised for our guilt and iniquities; the chastisement needful to obtain) peace and well-being for us was upon Him. And with He stripes (that wounded) Him we are healed and made whole (Isaiah 53:4–5 AMP).

Do we truly know what all happen to Jesus's body that day on the cross? Bleeding occurs when a blood vessel is damaged. If the vessel is internal, blood seeps into surrounding tissue, and a bruise forms. Where delicate blood vessels are near the surface of tissue, as they are in the nose, for example, a very slight injury or irritation may cause bleeding. For most people, minor bleeding causes no harm because the body soon stops it. It does this by three main mechanisms that act together. The nearby blood vessels contract and restrict the flow of blood to the area of the wound. The platelets in

---

[1] Nelson's Illustrated Bible Dictionary.
[2] The Blood Of Christ, Andrew Murray pg 88.

the blood gather where the blood vessels are damaged and stick to the vessel walls and each other to form a plug. In addition, interlacing strands of material called fibrin form in the damaged area.

Blood cells are then trapped in the fibrin mesh and form a clot that seals the break and the bleeding.[3] The blood platelets were all poured out of Jesus for us, which meant what poured out of Jesus was our healing for all the damaged areas of our life, He bridged the gap. The blood perfectly restores our rightful place with Him. When we take time to meditate and pray upon the power of that blood, appropriating it by faith for we will obtain a wonderful view of the liberty by which we can now have fellowship with God. Oh, the divine and wonderful power of the blood of Jesus! Through it, we can enter into the Holy Place, right there with Him. The blood pleads for us, and in us, with an eternal, unceasing effect. It removes sin from God's sight and from our conscience. Every moment we have full freedom, full entrance, and must remember that God has an open-door policy. Let us remember the blood above the doorframe of our house and the Passover.

The Lord will keep you free from every disease. He will not inflict on you the horrible diseases you knew in Egypt, but he will inflict them on all who hate you (Dt. 7:15 Thompson Chain Reference Bible). The blood of Jesus was poured out to act on our behalf to remove our fleshly sins from death and to protect the container of the Spirit (our body) from being polluted by Satan and his thoughts that cause us to sin. Often, people wonder why they are not being healed at a particular time that they want it. They must remember that what's been done to heal us has already taken place. While at Levi's house, Jesus was having dinner with many tax collectors and sinners, and the disciples asked, "Why does he eat with tax collectors and sinners?"

On hearing this, Jesus said to them, "It is not the healthy, who need a doctor, but the sick I have not come to call the righteous, but sinners" (Mark 2:17, Thompson Chain Reference Bible). God has made a promise with thou that diligently hearken to His voice.

---

[3] Family Medical Guide, pg 431.

> "And said, If thou wilt diligently hearken to the voice of the LORD thy God, and wilt do that which is right in his sight, and wilt give ear to his commandments, and keep all his statues, I will put none of these diseases upon thee, which I brought upon the Egyptians: for I am the LORD that healeth thee" (Exodus 15:26 KJV).

We can see that the key to divine healing is to diligently hearken to the voice of the Lord. One is not to seek or serve other gods.

> "Thou shalt not bow down to their gods, nor serve them, nor do after there works: but thou shalt utterly overthrow them, and quite break down their images. And you shall serve the LORD your GOD, and he shall bless thy bread, and thy water, and I will take sickness away from the midst of thee" (Exodus 23:24–25 KJV).

Within these two verses, we see a method that will lead to keeping diseases and sickness away from our bodies, be diligent to the voice of the Lord.

When someone gives us something as a blessing, we often wonder what the motive was behind why it was given to us. Jesus poured out His blood and He had a motive for doing it, so it was for healing and deliverance to get us into heaven to see our Father God and His greatness. After knowing Him intimately, we don't need to wonder what the motive is. Accepting the blood and believing that He can do what He says he will and that He is the I am that I am will get us into the Father's throne room. We can go in and out at will just to be in His presence or to get a hug. But not accepting what Jesus has done for us will keep us away from the throne room and out of the Lamb's Book of Life and thrown into the Lake of Fire (doom).[4]

---

[4] The blood of Christ, Andrew Murray.

The pollution of sin or the sense of defilement and impurity that sin brings to our inner being is what the blood cleanses.

[5]Cleaned, sanctified, and brought nigh by the power of the blood my earthly calling, my whole life, even my eating and drinking are a spiritual service. This will sanctify all of my work, business, money, house, and everything with which I have to do by the presence of God because I walk in His presence. Do we still need to ask if the blood can heal us? Jesus is more than one pint at a time, for He is enough for the whole world and doesn't need to wait to donate blood only every four months. He is the regenerator of life now and forever and ever Amen. Of all that is around us, TV, newspaper, books, and movies etc, we are saturated with false teaching. There is a God who we can depend on for truth. To understand God and the mystery of the Bible doesn't mean that God is not who he says that He is. There will always be false teachers around, so that is why Jesus came to teach, preach, and heal us. We are being forced to learn to things that are not true, so we must turn to God for all the answers. Understanding all the healing blood did for us will allow us to hook up to the transfusion process. This process will clear up all other teachings that don't line up with the word of God. God sent out the first teacher, His son, so that the teaching, preaching, and healing will be according to scripture. There is power in the words we used there can bring cursing or blessing. Jesus' body hung unashamed because there was no shame in His life. Jesus did no wrong but was crucified by unbelievers. That is still going on with us, but now we can operate the power to tell the forces of darkness to flee from our life. The body given to us is not our body it is God's to be used as protection while on the earth and exposed to sin. Jesus's body is our armor against the wiles of the Devil and His schemes. When we operate the sword of the word, all demons flee from our body.

---

[5]   The blood of Christ, Andrew Murray.

His Blood as a Transfusion for Our Life

[1]Scientists today are working to develop blood substitutes or artificial blood that could replace human blood in transfusions. Such research is very important because even with strict precautions, transfusions involve risk of reaction and the transmission of viruses and other infections through transfused blood. Scientific interest in blood probably began with the Greek physician Hippocrates, who lived during the 400 and 300 BC. He proposed that all diseases resulted from an imbalance of four humors (body fluids): black bile, blood, phlegm, and yellow bile. That theory led to bloodletting, the drawing of blood from a vein of a sick person so the disease would flow out with the blood. For many centuries, bloodletting was standard medical treatment Patients died from too much blood loss. [2]The only blood let out for our healing was when Jesus let out His pure blood for us. He told and warned everyone about what was going to happen when He died, that He shall return in three days. That sounds as though the truth is nothing but the blood of Jesus that can transfuse our life. When we say that our life is in a state or cycle of being deficient as a result of sickness or disease and not correctly in level with the way we want our life to be, then we are in the learning and knowledge state that there is a better way and I don't choose to live this way any longer. Somehow, one has to get to the point where

---

1   World book Encyclopedia "B" 75 anniversary edition.
2   Family Medical Guide, pg431.

they see their self doing wrong and where they notice that they are sinners will the healing began. If they notice they are doing wrong, then they know God. No one but God will make you notice that you have fallen short of the mark. The Blood of Christ will cleanse our consciences (Heb 9:14). One must go to the Father God and say, "Father God, I accept your blood that was sent to me thought your Son Jesus, I thank you and I want a total transfusion to take place in my life right now." There are three ways to get this transfusion: ask, seek, knock, and He shall open the door and let you in. What are you waiting for? One is so used to living the way they have been that if someone even mentions the fact of change they don't know how they will be able to get along. People learn differently throughout the different nations; we must all come together as one church family, one nation, and one blood. There is only one main blood bank, and you can bank on Jesus for the best blood transfusion. Our Father God is quick to multiply the blood loss to restore the flow. He also wants our hearts. I have donated blood before to save a life of another person, and the first thing they did was to test if the blood is okay for it to be passing from your body to someone else's. Donating is a wonderful feeling, and knowing that my blood cells are going to give life to someone else and the blood I have given will cause my body to regenerate new cells. When there is a blood donation into our bodies, what one must ask is "What has this blood been through?" Is the blood being donated from a born-again believer super charged with healing power? Jesus is the ultimate blood donor. We donate blood to save one person, but Jesus poured out his blood for all to be saved. Our blood is transferred to a bag and then stored; the blood is still alive within that bag. Notice that it is alive outside of our body, but then a reaction happens when it is put into the body and the breath of life blends with it. Jesus poured out his blood on the tree (or cross) for our container; the scripture says we are a vessel.

"From whom the whole body fitly joined together and compacted by that which every joint supplieth, according to the effectual working in the measure of every part maketh increase of the body unto the edifying of itself in love" (Eph 4:16 KJV). Being a donor is the pouring out of Jesus's love through you for someone else. The person that is being saved must be of the same blood type because blood of different types can't be mixed. Jesus is a universal donor for all to receive. Jesus's blood has a positive response to your needs in today's world.

> "I tell you the truth, unless you eat the flesh of the son of man and drink his blood; you have no life in you. Whoever eats my flesh and drinks my blood has eternal life, and I will raise him up at the last day. For my flesh is real food, and my blood is real drink. Whoever eats my flesh and drinks my blood remains in me, and I in him. Just as the living father sent me and I live because of the father, so the one who feeds on me will live because of me. This is the bread that came down from heaven. Your forefathers ate manna and died, but he who feeds on this bread will live forever" (John 6:53–58 NIV, Thompson Chain Reference Bible).

Jesus said whoever drinks my blood has eternal life. Jesus's blood was without sin and pure.[3] "Blood serves as a fluid highway, carrying food, oxygen, disease-fighting cells, and hormones (chemical messengers) throughout the body. It also carries away wastes for disposal. How do we replace worn-out blood components? Each formed element can live only a particular length of time, and so your body must continuously replace worn out cells. Red blood cells live about 120 days and platelets about 10 days; the life span of white blood cells varies greatly. Platelets stick to the edge of the cut and to one another forming a plug that will stop the bleeding. One could say that this is a bridge of healing, across the wounded or cut area." Our mind is a vital area where the healing takes place, in our thoughts. Our blood flows (Jesus's anointing) from the heart to the mind, but we have a bypass in the blood flow or anointing and that is our mouth.

---

[3] 1982 World book Encyclopedia, B volume 2.

Words are alive; they were activated with the breath of life, receiving both the words and the breath together. Speak the healing, for we have been given that power because of the blood and all the active elements of life. Speak your healing from the heart, not the mind; speak it right from the source of the blood. Before the Devil plants thoughts in your mind of how you are not worthy and causes strife in your life, speak the activity of the blood power fresh from the heart.[4] Use the blood nutrient that only Jesus poured out. The voice of the blood will not speak simply to teach us or to awaken thought; the blood speaks with divine and life-giving power. What it commands, it bestows, it works out in us the same disposition that was in our Lord Jesus. By His own blood, Jesus sanctifies us that we, holding nothing back, might surrender ourselves with all our hearts to the holy will of God. Everything that we have been through and experienced so far is moving us forward when the blood of Jesus cleans the inside of our heart. This total removal of everything that is stopping us from standing with Jesus at the Father's throne has been flushed out of our heart.

> "Paul asked some of the disciples, 'Did you receive the Holy Spirit when you believed?' They answered, 'No we have not even learned there is a Holy Spirit.' So Paul asked, 'Then what baptism did you receive?' 'John's baptism,' they replied. Paul said, 'John's baptism of repentance, he told the people to believe in the one coming after him, that is Jesus.' On hearing this, they were baptized into the name of the Lord Jesus. When Paul placed his hand on them the Holy Spirit came on them" (Act 19:1–6 NIV).

Our heart will then be filled with the blood that purifies and that is with the Holy Spirit's power operating in our blood. We are now ready to let out words from our mouth that have been sanctified

---

4   The blood of Jesus, Andrew Murray.

by God. Activating the words of the Gospel from our heart will not let the Devil have a chance to get to the words we speak. We will now operate and pray with tongues a language not known to the Devil. All of God's provisions depend on the condition of the heart. What condition was God's heart in when He sent his son?

Removing of Impurities

An impurity means something that is not pure, but has a fault. When we allow the Holy Spirit to operate in our lives, we start a process of Spiritual fire that burns within us. The Holy Spirit is always alive and active, but we have to choose to let the Holy Spirit operate in our lives. When we have complete thoughts of Jesus and we don't let the things of the earth influence us, by totally giving God our best, we operate in the blessing of the inheritance. We help ourselves so that the fire doesn't go out but burns with a new type of fuel. Satan wants us to be fueled with carbon and junk food. The devil's fuel will keep us in an environment that affects the body and blood. Negative thoughts induce bad blood enzymes that act like a cancer. When we choose the Holy Spirit's fuel, we choose to operate on a pure fuel that doesn't add junk to our body and plug our veins off from the blood flow. This fuel removes and burns out what is not needed, and we get to the point of completely cutting off the devil's fuel from our life. Believing is the first step to the purification stage of our lives. Taking Jesus into our heart is the second step. We are now purified in Christ, white as a pure glowing fire. In Daniel, we see Shadrach, Meshach, and Abednego being cast into the fiery furnace because they would not fall down and worship Nebuchadnezzar.

> "Then Nebuchadnezzar was full of fury and his facial expression was changed (to antagonism) against Shadrach, Meshach, and Abednego. Therefore he commanded that the furnace be heated seven times hotter than it was usually heated" (Daniel 3:19 AMP).

> "Then Nebuchadnezzar the king (saw and) was astounded, and he jumped up and said to his counselors. Did we not cast three men bound into the fire? They answered, True O king. He answered, behold. I see four men loose, walking in the midst of the fire, and they are not hurt! And the form of the fourth is like the son of GOD!" (Daniel 3:23–26 AMP).

It goes on to say that nothing was scorched and not even the smell of smoke clung to them, it also says that they were bound and then set free, four men are loose and walking in the midst fire. There was a protective shield with them that looked like the son of God. If we trust in God, we can rest assured that the smell from the Lake of Fire in the end times will not be anywhere around us.

> "But who can endure the day of his coming? And who can stand when He appears? For He is like a refiner's fire and like fullers' soap; 3 He will sit as a refiner and purifier of silver, and He will purify the priests, the sons of Levi, and refine them like gold and silver, that they may offer to the Lord offering in righteousness" (Malachi 3:2–3 AMP).

We all have sinned in our life; these are impurities that the devil is getting us to believe that we need to have to live in this world. The devil poisons us with sin.[1] Blood poisoning, or septicemia; this is not a single disease. It is a condition that is caused by the spread of a bacterial infection in your blood. The poison is either the bacteria that is causing the infection or poisonous substances called toxins that are made by the bacteria. But we are not of this world and not of the conditions of it. Only when we except the Lord as our savior and

---

[1] Family medical guide, pg 428 blood poisoning.

we are born again of the Spirit, then are we hooked in to the power of the Body of Christ.

Let us look at conditions of the body when a fever comes on, this is a temperature control; it is to raise the body heat up to fight off or burn off impurities that are trying to attack the body. We are to pray for the right temperature and not go beyond what it takes to burn off the impurities that are on us at that point God is the thermostat control, He wants to burn the impurities off our bodies, and at the same time, we are saying fever be gone to the control system and not letting the proper purification process take place. Let us remember that there is one place the heat is turned up and that is through the baptism of the Holy Spirit with fire. We must do our part to start this regeneration process through prayer.

Regeneration is only found in Matt 19:28 and Titus 3:5. This word literally means a "new birth" The Greek word so rendered (palingenesia) is used by classical writers with reference to the changes produced by the return of spring. In Matt 19:28, the word is equivalent to the "restitution of all things" (Acts 3:21). In Titus 3:5, it denotes that change of heart elsewhere spoken of as a passing from death to life (1 John 3:14); a renewal of the mind (Rom. 12:2); a resurrection from the dead (Eph. 2:6); a being quickened (2:1, 5). This change is ascribed to the Holy Spirit It originates not with man but with God (John 1:12, 13; 1 John 2:29, 5:1, 4). As to the nature of the change, it consists in the implanting of a new principle or disposition in the soul; the impartation of spiritual life to those who are by nature "dead in trespasses and sins."

First, God formed man in His image and then from the dust of the ground (so a body was formed). Next breathed into his nostrils the breath of life; the breath made man became a living soul. A body was formed but without life until the breath was given to activate life and get the blood moving and the body temperature regulated right to create a reactive force. Only God knows the time between the body and the breath. Man started giving the devil something that the devil didn't have possession of in the beginning, and the devil uses man against himself. We are to let the Lord fuel us with the words that He has spoken and not let the devil fuel us and twist the words with trash talk. This wrong use of words pollutes God's word and anything around that will change or alter the flow, even plug or dam up the flow of the blood of Jesus.

One of the ways the blood flow is cut off is through the eating of fat. So why does the Bible tell us to refrain from partaking of the fat of animals? Is it really a poison to the body? Is it a sin against God? Just think about it for a moment and ask yourself what are the consequences of eating the fat of animals? What about the results on the body? Does it damage the body? The answer is yes. We must remember that everything on this earth works according to seed time and harvest. Therefore, when we ingest the fat of animals, we must consider what seeds are being sown and what would the harvest of that crop look like? If fat, like sin, can be damaging to the body, then where are we to draw the line? Is a little sin okay? Maybe even well for us? No. The truth is that saturated fat (sin) does harm the body and eventually leads to death because of the reduction of the blood flow. It is true that certain oils are essential to sustain the body and promote good health, but they are not even in the same category as saturated fat. Think about it as fleshly beings that must operate in the world. Like those oils, it is a necessary element of our survival. Choosing sin, on the other hand, like eating saturated fats, is simply a dangerous response to temptation, an indulgence in the forbidden simply because it is available and appealing to the senses. In other words, it tastes good. Scientists warn us about the dangerous effect of saturated fats just like God warns us about the consequences of sin.[2] Define saturated fats as such, "Saturated fats are the characteristically hard fatty meat, as well as in vegetable oil such as coconut and palm. We usually consider all saturated fats as bad fats—and most are. Some saturated fats may turn out not to be as harmful as others. For the sake of simplicity, we suggest…that all saturated fats be considered essentially the same." Just like sin. Look what happens if the message taught from the altar is not prepared right.

---

[2]   Dr. William P. Castelli and Glen C. Griffin, Good Fat Bad Fat.

"The sons of Eli were base and worthless;
they did not know or regard the Lord. And the
custom of the priests with the people was this:
when any man offered sacrifice, the priest's servant came while the flesh was boiling with a flesh
hook of three prongs in his hand: and he thrust
it into the pan or kettle or caldron or pot; all that
the flesh hook brought up the priest took for himself. So they did in Shiloh with all the Israelites
who came there. Also, before they burned the fat,
the priest's servant came and said to the man who
sacrificed, Give the priest meat to roast, for he
will not accept boiled meat from you, but raw.
And if the man said to him, Let them burn the
fat first, and then you may take as much as you
want, the priest's servant would say, No! Give it
to me now or I will take it by force. So the sin of
the (two) young men was very great before the
Lord, for they despised the offering of the Lord"
(1 Samuel 2:12–17).

One would wonder in today's world if the three-pronged flesh
hook is reprehensible of the devil's pitch fork known to carnal man.
There are so many pastors that are preparing their notes for a sermon
and they are not asking God for a revelation from the word of God.
Some pastors are serving an unprepared dinner to the congregation
by reaching in before the Lord finished all the preparation in their
heart.

"Why then do you kick (trample upon,
treat with contempt) my sacrifice and my offering which I commanded, and honor your sons
above me by fattening yourselves upon the choic-
est part of every offering of my people Israel?"
(1 Samuel 2:29).

Saturated fats vary; however, overall they are dangerous and promote death. There will always be some fat in the body of Christ, until that day when we receive our new body. Unfortunately, too many of us are already living completely saturated lives. We all know that it is easy to get caught up in sin if we are not careful to heed to the instructions of God. Addiction is the perfect example. So many people start out compromising the findings of God in little ways, like saying to them that little bit won't hurt. Then before they know it, they become addicted and lose their ability to limit themselves. In the same way that cholesterol from saturated fat slowly poisons the blood supply to the body and damages the human heart, sin also poisons the flow of the life substance from heaven and damages the human "spiritual heart." The best way to preserve the heart is simply to turn from saturated fat (sin) to deny it access to the body. Sometimes, it is hard to resist temptations like ice cream, potato chips, candy, etc. Succumbing to these temptations over and over again is costly to the flow of the blood in our body that does so much for us. It is our bodies that keep the Holy Spirit within. Thank God that he knows the nature of our struggles. Through the sacrifice of Jesus Christ, He made Himself available to us, and we can rest assured that help is always only a prayer away.

> "And the Lord spake to Moses, saying, Speak into the children of Israel, saying ye shall eat no matter of fat, of ox, or of sheep, or of goats" (Leviticus 7:22–23 NIV).

The question I want to ask is "How much fat did God say not to eat?"

The answer is no matter of fat. There is a direct correlation between the amount of sin (fat) in someone's life and the health of his life substance (blood) and the condition of the man's spirit (heart). The Lord spoke to me very clearly when I chose to write about blood, the body effects, and the food we eat, also the way we treat our earthly body as well as our spiritual body; He said that saturated fat represents sin.

"But Abel brought fat portions from some
of his firstborn of his flock" Gen 4:4 NIV).

Thus, He requires the sin offering, not for himself, but for the benefit of those He loves. The Lord is also specific enough about the process of such offerings in order that His children should readily choose the portion that is good for them. If He took the worst part (sin) for Himself and gave the rest back into our hands, why then is it so hard for people to simply follow instructions? Why do we find it so hard to trust Him? After all, he is our Father. He knows that sin leads to death. He knows that like animas fat, sin is bad for the body, and He does everything He can to direct us away from sin and get us to eat from the master's table. He made the choice very simple. Life or death! He even insisted that to choose life that it would be better for those who would struggle with the decision, and still, the body of Christ rebels. Like choosing to eat fat of animals against God's warning, the children of God also choose to entertain sin against His will. If not for the mercy of God, sin would have already destroyed humanity. Instead He continues to offer every new generation the opportunity to experience the fullness of the benefits of the sin offering no matter how many times the people have ignored His instruction. Sin will always find a way to mess up our lives. It will keep clogging arteries, slowing down the body circulation, and overwhelming the hearts of men, so that blood and healing is affected. The only way to rid the body of that kind of spiritual fat is to expose it, expel it from our lives, and thoroughly avoid it in the future. According to the Word of God, the Lord's desire for his children is to live prosperously. How do we achieve prosperity?

We achieve prosperity by making choices that line up with the instructions of God. First, we must get rid of that which is not meat Second we must repent for blocking the flow with the fat of sin and third, we much get serious about the Word of God. The Lord tells us that the Word of God is sharper than any two-edged sword. It is supernaturally designed to cut right through any fat that might attach itself to the body of Christ. Ultimately, we must completely put our lives into the hands of our Creator and choose to live for

Him instead of for ourselves. Because we are not our own, we belong to Him.

> "Then cometh the end, when He shall have delivered up the kingdom to God, even to the Father; when he shall put down all rule and all authority and power" (1 Coro 15:24 KJV).

I believe that Jesus will be handing over the best cut of USDA top choice meat ever!

God himself will have trimmed off the fat that the devil tried to put on the body of Christ. He is our protection against the enemy simply because we trust in Him completely. Satan, on the other hand, knows that death is inevitable. His goal is to block or dam the circulation of life substance in the body and steal, kill, and destroy the blessings of God right out from under our noses. He is anti-Christ. He desires only death for the bride of Christ because he knows that to destroy her would destroy humanity and endlessly grieve the very heart of God. God wants the best for us, which is why he sent the blood. Fortunately for us, we already know the end of the story! Salvation is the blessing from which comes our power and strength. It is not of this world it is of God, His only Begotten Son is the way to the Father. Satan has only the power and authority that we surrender to him. His fierce threats and seductive influences are merely imitations of the deadly weapons he claims them to be. They have no real power to defeat the children of God. This scripture tells us that the fat-trimming process begins by dealing with the fat on the innermost parts. Is there fat (sin) covering your inner parts? Since the Lord cleans us up from the inside out, we can rest assured that He will direct us in the ways we should live. He proclaims.

> "But he answered and said, 'It is written, Man shall not live by bread alone, but by every word that proceeds out of the mouth of God'" (Matt 4:4 NIV).

Also don't forget the wine (blood) offer up for us. The Word of God makes it very clear that the peace offering itself begins with dealing with the inner parts.

> "And if his obligation be a sacrifice of peace offering, if he offer it of the herd; whether it be a male or a female, he shall offer it without blemish before the Lord. And he shall lay his hand upon the head of his offering, and kill it at the door of the tabernacle of the congregation; and Aaron's son the priests shall sprinkle the blood upon the altar round about. And he shall offer the sacrifice of the peace offering an offering made by fire unto the Lord; the fat that covereth the inwards, and all the fat unto the Lord; the fat that covereth the inwards, and all the fat that is upon the inwards, and the two kidneys, and the fat that is on them, which is by the flanks, and the caul above the liver, with the kidneys, it shall be taken away. An Aaron's son shall burn it upon the altar upon the burnt sacrifice, which is upon the wood that is upon the fire; it is an offering made by fire, of a sweet savor unto the Lord" (Lev 3:1–5 KJV).

A sweet savor unto the Lord. Wow, can you just imagine the joy that the Father receives as fat that pushes against the flow of the blood is cleared from our life and the healing takes place. Lord, thank you for doing the trimming and showing us how to maintain the body's health.

The Lord knows where the fat is attached to the animal before his inner parts are even exposed. He knows what part is to be burned by fire. He instructs that all the fat covering the inner parts or connected to the kidneys, along with the fat near the loins and covering the liver, are to be removed first, and then burned by Aaron's sons on the altar. There is to be a burnt offering made by fire which the Lord proclaim to be a very pleasing aroma to him. Removing fat removes pressure from veins and arteries and allows free flowing of the blood; remember when the Lord sets you free you are free in deed. But extra fat on the body can absorb elements that need to be put in the direction of healing. I went shopping at the local grocery store, and passing the meat department, I started to think about how the butcher trims the fat off the meat before he weights it, wraps it up, and puts it out before the people to purchase. I considered how sometimes customers rebel when they have to pay for cuts of meat containing too much fat. People really do know that the value of fat compares much less than the value of the meat. I also noticed the butcher dated the meat for freshness. Many people have jobs where they are responsible for making sure that the food we eat is healthy. For example, dietitians that work at hospitals have to specially prepare food so that their patients get the proper nutritional value. Why? It promotes healing. When our Father God prepares a meal for us, we are served substance that nourishes and rejuvenates the soul. It is eternal food, for once we accept Christ as our Savior, and we still need extra energy and provision to fight off the devil and what he tries to throw at us. We are all born hungry for something and looking for who is going to feed us. As babies, we suckle milk from our mother's breast, but we grow, we must learn to chew our solid food. In the realm of the Spirit, the Word of God is the solid food of mature Christians. Everyone knows that good food and exercise are the best combination to promote health. Good exercise circulates more blood through the body. Exercising our power and authority in Christ after savoring the rich morels of the Word of God is the best way to utilize our swords and armor, especially if we commit to the same routines until they become habit. Think about the Lord's Supper where Jesus sat at the table with His disciples and intimately dined with them.

"For the bread of life is he that comes down from Heaven, and gives life to the world" (John 6:33). We don't need any more substance than that, but God knows that it takes us a while to grasp the miracle of that great sacrifice of everything that Jesus went through, and the blood poured out for us. Just like with the Old Testament offerings, the fat (sin) was separated from the body of Christ and offered up to God. Then things changed; we moved from meat to the Bread of Life. Let us remember the Lord's Supper and what He proclaimed.

> "The Lord proclaims, 'I tell you the truth. Unless you eat the flesh of the son of man and drink his blood, you have no life in you. Whoever eats my flesh and drinks my blood has eternal life, and I will raise him up at the last day'" (John 6:53).

Notice that in the content of the Lord's message, He no longer focuses on meat. He also focuses on the blood that gives life. He doesn't have to just focus on the meat of the word because He has already introduced to us the Bread of Life.

Total Oneness with
Our Savior

When I went to church as a little boy, I knew that there was a God, great and powerful. I heard people talk about a wonderful God, and I often wondered why things happened in a certain order, why only it seemed to be the holiest ones that were partaking in the good things of God. I felt as if I was not at the fullness of God with my relationship and had often thought of what it took to get to know more. I yearned inside to know and to be closer; there were a lot of things I had learned about what God did from words of other Christians. I felt as though God was watching over me and did know that I could get closer and have a relationship with Him. One can get caught up in the worldly things around us and be pulled directions other than a relationship with Him. When we called upon the name of the Lord to be our Savior and to come into our hearts, we had to think about it before the thought of saying or the action of doing it came into our mouths. This is meditation of the word, we need to mix it with prayer and receive from God and then go do the works God placed within us.

"Because if you acknowledge and confess with your lips that Jesus is Lord and in your heart believe (adhere to, trust in, and rely on the truth) that God raised Him from the dead, you will be saved. For with the heart a person believes (adhere to, trusts in, and relies on Christ) and

70

so is justified (declared righteous, acceptable to God), and with the mouth he confesses (declares openly and speaks out freely his faith) and confirms (his) salvation" (Romans 10:9–10 KJV).

Keeping ourselves totally being in relationship with God means to lay ourselves all down and let God do the work in us, so that we can go among the earth and spread the good news of our Savior. This is a reproduction process. God said to reproduce and multiply and replenish the earth. He said replenish it; he wants us to replenish it the way it was produced once already. By speaking against what the blood was poured out for, we activate negative forces that work the opposite way that God meant for them to be activated. When some sickness or disease has us down, spreading the good news and making sure that we are helping others to get their name written in the book of life is harder to do. In this world, we search for oneness with something and someone else if we don't put God first. Oneness of the marriage between husband and wife is a day to day willingness to be closer than the day before. We want to feel loved, but must remember that love is not a feeling; the feeling is the result of love. Love is unconditional; let us thank God for not putting a condition on His love for us. The love of Jesus also is unconditional.[1] When Jesus was tempted, He had to maintain his love and show how perfect His will was surrendered to the holiness of God. We have seen that total holiness in man is when he is in perfect oneness will Jesus that will put us at the throne with God the Father. He sanctified himself to be in perfect oneness with the will of God. We often say, "Lord, if you will do this for me, then I will worship you." We make a deal or put a condition back on our love for our Lord. Whether we believe or don't believe, Jesus's blood is still active and I would like to know that the blood of Jesus is moving on my behalf. Why are there so many things to distract us? If our thoughts sway away from the worship (war-ship) of Jesus, then we have left our post or dropped our weapon and our defenses are open. Only then we are giving the devil the Glory and not God.

---

[1] The blood of Jesus, Andrew Murray.

God made a blood covenant with us by sending his only begotten son to restore life's connection to us and to bridge the gaps of our wounds and cuts, so the healing takes place. He fills our post for us. He reattached himself to the tree, willingly lying down and He has the power to take Himself up again. When Eve was amidst the garden, she offered Adam the forbidden fruit after the serpent convinced her she would not die. The fruit was removed from its (Blood) life source. Eve offered Adam a dying process. Death happened because the wages of sin is death. What it is saying here is that we must stay connected to the vine that the Blood of Jesus flows through. God will save us from the ruler of darkness as long as we make the right choice to follow Jesus. Look at the scripture below; it says let us have complete authority over all the earth. One gets complete authority by being made in the image and likeness of the Father, Son, and Holy Spirit, and not leaving one of these elements out. Power and authority comes in remembering from whom we were made by believing and accepting Him as Lord. Jesus helped our bodies here on earth, but we will receive a new heavenly body.

> "God said, 'Let us (Father, Son, and Holy Spirit,) make mankind in Our image, after Our likeness, and let them have complete authority over the fish of the sea, the birds of the air, the (tame) beasts, and over all the earth, and over everything that creeps upon the earth'" (Gen 1:26 AMP).

When you look in the mirror, you see yourself as an image, read it again, what it says, mankind was made in the image, the key words here are "in the image." In means, we are in Him, not just a reflection, but we are to reflect with his love He gave us from the inside out. "And when he was entered into a ship, his disciples followed him. And, behold, there arose a great tempest in the sea, insomuch that the ship was covered with the wave: but he was asleep. And his disciples came to him, and awake him, saying, Lord save us: we parish" (Matt 8:23–25 NIV).

While there was a storm, the water was rough and they could not see their image in the mirrored reflection of the smooth water and they didn't remember from whose image they were made and whose blood they have accepted. When Jesus calmed the sea, the reflection of remembrance came back to them. Now we receive the Father through the Son, along with the Holy Spirit's power, this comes from being born again. We are to die ourselves and then be healed unto a new creation; a new creation is from something that doesn't exist as of yet. You don't get to be a new creation from old things that were created already, without new blood cells of purification we still are lost. It's a free gift, but yet people are saving up gold, silver, animal offering, etc., for it, saying, "Well, when the time is right I will worship Jesus." They are worshipping things that are earthly vessels.

> "Neither is new wine put in old wineskins;
> for if it is, the skins burst and are torn in pieces,
> and the wine is spilled and the skins are ruined.
> But new wine is put into fresh wineskins, and so
> both are preserved" (Matt 9:17 KJV).

It's says the old skin will tear of burst if new wine enters into it The container was already conditioned for the wine that has been put in it. If one doesn't have the Lord in their life, they feel as though they are ruined and about to burst and not in the right condition to receive the new wine from heaven. That is why we are to be healed and made a new creation, to be able to accept the new wine that He has for us. The wine represents the blood of Jesus. If we remain in our old form, what will happen? We will not have our name written in the Lamb's Book of Life. He wants to preserve us in eternity with Him.

> "Verily, Verily, I say unto you, He that belie-
> veth on me, the works that I do shall he do also;
> and greater works than these shall he do, because
> I am go unto my Father" (John 14:12 KJV).

It says greater works than Him shall one do if they believe and accept everything He has done for us to the pouring out of the blood for us, only after Jesus went to the father. He sent greater things because He was with the Father. Jesus left us charged up with what He had at the time and then went to visit the Father to get us super-charged with power from on high. If we are aware of all that the blood can do for us, how much more is he talking about when he says greater works than these shall we do? This is an awesome state-ment to meditate on, greater because he is coming to the wedding.

"On the third day there was a wedding at Cana of Galilee, and the mother of Jesus was there. Jesus also was invited with His disciples to the wedding. And when the wine was all gone, the mother of Jesus said to Him they have no more wine! Jesus said to her, (Dear) woman what is that to you and me? (What do we have in common? Leave it to me) my time (hour to act) has not yet come. His mother said to the servants, whatever He says to do it. Now there were six water pots of stone standing there, as the Jewish custom of purification (ceremonial washing) demanded, holding twenty to thirty gallons apiece. Jesus said to them fill the water pots with water, so they fill them up to the brim. Then he said to them, Draw out now take it to the manager of the feast (to the one presiding, the superintendent of the banquet) so they took him some. And when the manager tasted the water just now turned into wine, not knowing where it came from—though the servants who had drawn the water knew-he called the bridegroom" (John 2:1–9 AMP).

Jesus's first miracle was changing the water into wine at the wedding. There is an ultimate wedding planned. Our bodies are 95 percent water, and He wants to change it to new wine before the wedding comes.

> "Let us rejoice and be glad and give him glory! For the wedding of the Lamb has come, and his bride has made herself ready" (Rev 19:7).

The Lord will be coming for a bride, the church to the ultimate wedding with his people who have accepted the blood and the power of it The blood flows through the body, and we are members of His body. If we are members, then his blood is flowing through us. Think of that for a minute or take as long as you would like, Jesus's blood flows through us. This is when we truly realize the fullness of His blessings. When we set the dining table to eat, we typically use plates and silverware and plastic cups.

When we invite friends over to eat, however, we sometimes set the table differently. We might put on a table cloth, use the good plates and silverware, and trade in those plastic cups for glasses. Now what if God the Father was to show up for dinner? Would we need to use gold-tipped glasses? No. God isn't concerned about our silverware and glasses. He is only concerned with the heart. What if God Himself was to set the table? Would he use the fine china? Would he lay out beautiful linen napkins? Would he provide beautiful wine glasses for that new wine and platter for the bread of life? What would it smell like? Would the aroma of heaven fill the whole room, and would God choose to serve to his children the best cut of meat? The answer is yes! Of course, this is a true statement.

"Oh Father you prepare a table for us in the mist of our enemies, and how sweet that aroma is. Thou preparest a table before me in the presence of mine enemies: thou anointest my head with oil; my cup runneth over" (Psalms 23:5 NIV). He makes our cup runneth over to share with others the blessings. It implores His goodness and mercy to follow us where we go; His plan has always been and will always be to give us meat for today and seeds to plant for the harvests of the futures. Why, it's simple. Because he loves us first!

Dining with God is better than going to Grandma's house for dinner. Things I liked about Grandma's house were that I remember how we used to call ahead of time to let Grandma know we were coming. When we arrived at Grandma's, there were scented cinnamon apple candles on the tables, beautiful throw rugs on the floor, and an old deck of cards was set out on the coffee table in case somebody wanted to play a game of rummy. Grandma knew we were coming, and she lovingly prepared her entire home for our visits. She made sure that we had everything we needed. If we decided to spend the night, there were goose down pillows and comforters to keep us nice and warm at night. She kept the temperature in the house just right, and there were family pictures and photo albums everywhere. (What would God's photo album of our life look like?) She sure could cook too. Grandma's house was filled with the aroma of good old-fashioned home cooking. Our Father has a place better than Grandma's house prepared for each of us. In my Father's house, there are many rooms. He knows the desires of our hearts and He hears our cries for help when we need. Believe it or not, the meal he has prepared for us surpasses even that of Grandma's special recipes. God prepared a special recipe for our life through the Bible and telling the truth about His Son. He guides our life to bring us into His presence.

> "Ye cannot drink the cup of the Lord,
> and the cup of devils; ye cannot be partakes
> of the Lord's Table and the table of devils"
> (1 Corinthians 10:21 KJV).

Also the aroma of love, agape love, fills the air to let us know that we are home. There is always hope, provision, comfort, grace, healing, and so much more with us and present at the Lord's Table. All we have to do is call ahead of time and let Him know that we're coming home for dinner; we have invited your son Jesus into our heart and He showed us the way into true healing. Jesus made our heart flow with blood and emotions again and removes the hardness of hatred for our brothers and sister to so we can help guide them to the Father's house with us. I truly believe that the meal prepared for us is not to be looked at, but to know that the aroma of it is sufficient as it enters our airway and removes the undesired aromas of this world, and then enters into our bloodstream and heal us just by the aroma. All through this writing about the blood, we see the need of eating right with our fleshly body, and also eating with our spiritual body. There are different things that affect the blood, we have seen and learned about some of the blood operations in our bodies, and what some of the activities of the blood and the heart of man there are. But through it all, it should give you a better understanding of why we need Jesus to be our guide and deliverer. I have come to grips with what it takes to get to the heavenly place prepared for me. Confess with your mouth and believe in your heart and be a doer of the word, not just a hearer. Circulate the blood just don't stay dormant. The children of God must openly rebuke the obvious as well as the subtle influences of Satan and his opposition, lest they jeopardize their own provisions set up for them. For surely, the double-minded man will be cast away from the table of the Lord and fellowship with His family. We are to love God with all of our hearts, our entire mind, and all of our soul. It seems like such a simple request, but the truth is, that no man has ever been able to fulfill the requirement of all. Yet in spite of our inadequacy, God has redeemed us through His son and paved the way to redemption for us. We've been given so much, and now it is time to stop wasting time about getting to the provision of God. It is time for the children of God to start cleaning up their act because it is more than an act, it is a script designed by God. It is time they start trimming the spiritual fat from their lives and get the body of Christ into shape in our life.

"Now Abel kept flocks, and Cain worked the soil. In the course of time Cain brought some of the fruits of the soil as an offering to the Lord. But Abel brought fat from some of the first-born of His flock. The Lord looked with favor on Abel's and His offering. But on Cain and his offering he did not look with favor. So Cain was very angry, and his face downcast Then the Lord said to Cain, 'Why are you angry? Why is your face downcast? If you do what is right, will you not be accepted? But if you do not do what is right, sin is crouching at your door; it desires to have you, but you must master it'" (Gen 4:5 NIV).

There was among his flock some just born again that needed the final trimming of some fat (sin) that was still on them, and for Abel to have a purified flock, this last process had to take place. He offered the fat of the firstborn of His flock, for this was to be the offering back to the Lord for all that He had done. When I offer myself back to the Lord, I will be washed by the blood and white as snow.

"Then one of the elders asked me, 'These in white robes, who are they and where did they come from?' I answered, 'Sir, you know' and he said, 'These are they that have come out of the great tribulation; they have wash their robes and made them white in the blood of the lamb'" (Rev 7:13–14 KJV).

Let's look at the colors of the Bible and what being washed white as snow means.

"Then there is the white of purification. The white of the robes of righteousness. Let us be glad and give him the glory! For the wedding of the lamb has come, and his bride has made herself ready. Fine linen, bright and clean was given her to wear. (Fine linen stands for righteous act of saints)" (Rev 19:7–8).

The White
Represents light

"And days after this, Jesus took with Him Peter and James and John his brother, and led them up on a high mountain by themselves. And his appearance under-went a change in the presence; and His face shone clear and bright like the sun, and His clothing became as white as light And behold, there appeared to them Moses, and Elijah, who kept talking with Him. Then peter begin to speak and said to Jesus, Lord it is good and delightful that we are here; it you approve, I will put up three booths here-one for you and one for Moses and one for Elijah. While he was still speaking a shining cloud (composed of light) overshadowed them, and a voice from the cloud said, This is my Son, My beloved, with Whom I am (and have always been) delighted. Listen to Him! When the disciples heard it, they fell on their faces and were seized with alarm and struck with fear. But Jesus came and touched them and said, Get up, and do not be afraid. And when they raised their eyes, they saw no one but Jesus only" (Matt 17:2–8 AMP).

"White is the horse that will carry a rider that is faithful and true. Then I fell prostrate at his feet to worship (to pay divine honors) to him, but he (restrained me) and said, refrain! (You must not do that!) I am (only) another servant with you and your brethren who have (accepted and hold) the testimony borne by Jesus. Worship God! For the substance (essence) of the truth revealed by Jesus is the spirit of all prophecy (the vital breath, the inspiration of all inspired preaching and interpretation of divine will and purpose, including both mine and yours) After that I saw heaven opened, and behold, a white horse (appeared)! The One who was riding it is called Faithful (trustworthy), Loyal, Incorruptible, Steady and True, and He has a title (name) inscribed Which He alone knows or can understand he is dressed in a robe dyed by dipping in blood, and the title by which He is called is The Word of God. And the troops of heaven, Clothed in fine linen, dazzling and clean, followed Him on white horse. From His mouth goes forth a sharp two edged sword with which He can smite (afflict, strike) the nations; and He will shepherd and control them with a staff (scepter, rod) of iron. He will tread the winepress of the fierceness of the winepress of the fierceness of the wrath and indignation of God the All-Ruler (the Almighty, the Omnipotent). And on His garment (robe) and on His thigh He has a name (title) inscribed, king of kings and lord of lords (Rev 20:10–16).

White is also the color of the great white throne.

"Then I saw a great white throne and the One Who was seated upon it, from whose presence and from the sight of whose face earth and sky fled away, and no place was found for them. I saw the dead, great and small; they stood before the throne, and books were opened, which is (the book) of life, and the dead were judged sentenced) by what they had done (their whole way of feeling and acting, their aims and endeavors) in accordance with what was recorded in the books. And the sea delivered up the dead who were in it, death and Hades (the state of death or disembodied existence) surrendered the dead in them, and all were tried and their cases determined by what they had done (according to their motives, aims, and works). Then death and Hades (the state of death or disembodied existence) were thrown into the lake of fire. This is the second death, the lake of fire, and if anyone's (name) was not found recorded in the book of Life. He was hurled into the lake of fire."

We now should see what the importance of the blood of Jesus is, the fleshly start of our life and all that fire body is exposed to in its lifetime and be able to distinguish all the elements that can harm us. We also see that nutrients are all around us with a negative impact or the positive impact that will change our life forever and eternity, we do the best we can to be on the right road to God's throne room, but we fall short. We know what is right and we often do wrong. That is why the Blood of Jesus was poured out when He died on the tree (or cross) and said it is done. We were healed and that is that, just except what it says, for it is the truth. There is nothing but the blood of Jesus, and people choose to leave it out of their life. Why through interpretations of the Bible is the blood being left out?

Thank you! Thanks for the Blood of Jesus in our life, Father God. The day will come when the blood will not matter anymore because we are now in the heavenly realm with God. Our earthly body has passed away for we have a new body. This environment can never cause us to fall again.

Glossary

Anticoagulant Anemia. The condition in which there is a reduction of the number of red blood cells corpuscles or of the total amount of hemoglobin in the blood stream or of both, resulting in a paleness generalized weakness. Lack of vigor or vitality, and lifelessness.

Bone marrow. Active tissue that create rich blood cells, including all of the red cells and platelets and most of the white cells.

Chlorophyll. The blood of plant life that contains life-giving nutrients that are easily assimilated by the human body.

Cholesterol. A steroid-like chemical present in some foods, notably animal fats, eggs, and dairy products.

Electrolyte. Any substance which in solution or in liquid form is capable of conducting an electric current by the movement of its positive and negative ions to the electrolyte.

Enzyme. Various protein-like substances, formed in plant and animal cells, that act as organic catalysts in initiating or speeding up specific chemical reactions and that usually become inactive or unstable at high temperatures.

Fibrin. An insoluble protein formed in blood as it clots. Fibrin is the substance that unites blood cells to close any damage to blood vessel walls.

Hemoglobin. The red coloring matter of the red blood corpuscles of vertebrates, a protein-yielding heme and globin on hydrolysis; it carries oxygen from tire lungs to the tissues and carbon dioxide from the tissues to the lungs.

Hemolytic anemia. This is a disorder in which your red blood cells are destroyed prematurely. When this occurs, your body attempts to compensate by producing new red cells at a faster rate.

Immune system. Protection against something disagreeable or harmful.

Lymphocytes. A type of white blood cell that recognizes foreign cells, infectious agents, and other foreign substances and participate in the body's immune reaction against them.

Neutrophils. Most of the white blood cell which attacks and engulfs bacteria.

Nutrients. To nourish: anything nutritious.

Plasma. Fluid part of blood, as distinguished from the corpuscles used for transfusions.

Platelet. Any of certain round or oval, nonucleated disks, smaller than a red blood cell and containing no hemoglobin, found in the blood of mammals and associated with the process of blood clotting.

Red blood cells. The circulating blood cells that carry oxygen to the tissues and return carbon dioxide to the lungs.

Septicemia. Blood poisoning is not a single disease. It is a condition that is caused by the spread of bacterial infection in your blood.

Sickle cell anemia. An inherited disease from both parents, the red blood cells contain an abnormal hemoglobin in your red blood cells, called hemoglobin *S. Thalassemia*. A inherited defect that prevents the formation of normal amounts of hemoglobin A, the type of hemoglobin that is found in red blood cells after the first few months of life.

Thrombolytics. A drug that acts to dissolve blood clots.

White blood cells. Blood cells that protect the body against infection by destroying bacteria and producing antibodies.

Bibliography

Analytical Research labs Inc, 2225 W, Alice Ave, Phoenix, AZ, 85021. Tissue Mineral Analysis, 602-995-1580, Test 2005.

Andrew Murray, The Blood of Christ, Bethany House Publishers, Minneapolis Minnesota, 2001.

Bergeron, Biziak, and Brady, Medical Guide, Sixth Edition, Publisher Prentice Hall, Upper Saddle River, New Jersey, 07456, Copyright 2001.

Dake, Finis Jennings, God's Plan for Man, Duke Publishing Inc., Lawrenceville, Georgia, 1977.

Dr. S Brandon Moore, Mayo Medical School, Everything You Need to Know about Medical Test, Springhouse, 1996.

Issac Asimov, How Did We Find Out about Blood, Walker Publishing Co. INC. Copyright 1986.

King James Version of the Bible, PC Study Bible, V4.2b, Publisher Bible Soft, 2004.

Marilyn Hickey, The Power of the Blood. Marilyn Hickey Ministries, 1987.

Nature's Sunshine Products Inc, Product (Chlorophyll), Spanish Fork, Utah, 84660. 1-800-223-8225.

Nelson's Illustrated Bible Dictionary, PC Study Bible, V4.2b, Publisher Bible Soft, 2004.

Stephen Cumbaa, The Bones and Skeleton Book, Workman Publishing, New York, Oct 1991.

Steve Parker, Look at Your Body, Topic Bone Structure, Aladdin Books Ltd. 1996.

Strong, James, The New Strong's Exhaustive Concordance of the Bible, Thomas Nelson Publishers, Nashville, Tennessee, 1995.

The American Medical Association, Family Medical Guide, Publisher
    Random House, 1990.
World Challenge Inc, Time Square Church Pulpit Series, Feeding
    Christ, By David Wilkerson, Feb 13,2002.

About the Author

Delray's first big move of God was after those long walks with his sister to church in the snow and cold of Michigan, where he grew up, followed construction after his dad got him a job at a Dow-owned pumping station out of high school. Construction company was from Houston; the company's next job was in Kansas for a short period of time and later moved to the Victoria, Texas, area and then to Corpus Christi, Texas. Where it is his place of residence today, throughout all the moves realized all people have the same common problems and need Jesus.

After going to church all my life, but never felt that special move in the Spirit. Another move of God in his life was a walk the Emmaus Retreat, where he attended and later served, another big move was the Promise Keepers movement, 1995. Delray gave his heart to the Lord, and the relationship into the Spirit began. After attending Promise Keeper, Delray served at many conferences on the prayer team, 1997. Delray attended Stand in the Gap in Washington, DC, prayer for the nation. Serving at his local church as usher and master teacher of first through fifth grade class, later got involved with prison ministry and is still involved after fifteen years, attended Minnesota Graduate School of Theology and acquired a master's degree. Ordained through Cornerstone Church, Corpus Christi, Texas. Delray is happily married for thirty-two years and has wife, Sharon, and four children.

CPSIA information can be obtained
at www.ICGtesting.com
Printed in the USA
BVHW072157020321
601492BV00008B/799